C000157998

Praise for Take Coi
Spacecraft and Fly]

Congratulations Keith on writing 'Fly Back to Love.' I believe we each have a mission to help our world be less afraid and to evolve in the direction of love. I trust that your new book is part of this mission. – Robert Holden, author of 'Loveability' and 'Life Loves You'

Your passion and energy is leaping off these pages Keith! Love your take on the nature of thoughts. – Kahil

I love what I have been able to read so far. I cannot wait until the book is published. I will definitely be a buyer. Love your work. Many blessings and much success to you. – Anita

Loved this article. The breath and the celebrations are definitely part of the process. It took me quite some time to realize that unless you appreciate what you have accomplished, you'll never find the energy to keep going. Great read! – Robert Fuller at ThoughtfulTalkBlog.com

Love your posts. Keep them coming. A great, fresh new on our lives. Taking control is what we all want.–Tom "Big Al" Schreiter

Beautiful story and a good reminder to remember at progress may be being made in the midst of chall .ges. Thank you. – Rose

The things you say and every word so beautifu . fantastic pictures of life! I like it very much! Thank you! – ,   on

Congratulations and good luck with the publication o . .ur book. Your insight is appealing. I will definitely put your b ok on my list of 'to read' books. Thank you for sharing. – Steve Leasock, author of 'One Moment in Life'

I needed these words. It's very difficult to let go of these thoughts and belief systems that have been entrained on us since we were children, but I know it's possible. Just takes some work. Thanks, Keith! – Jonathin

A wise discourse of insight that inspires faith in humanity again. – Gerald

I love your writings . . . they go straight to my heart. It's been a long time since I enjoyed reading that much. – Lene

Take Control of Your Spacecraft and Fly Back to Love

Keith
Higgs

A Manual and Guidebook for Life's Journey

#Personal Growth
#Spirituality

Copyright © 2016 by Keith Higgs.

Library of Congress Control Number:		2016914118
ISBN:	Hardcover	978-1-5245-9403-9
	Softcover	978-1-5245-9402-2
	eBook	978-1-5245-9401-5

All rights reserved. No part of this book may be reproduced or transmitted in any form or by any means, electronic or mechanical, including photocopying, recording, or by any information storage and retrieval system, without permission in writing from the copyright owner.

Print information available on the last page.

Rev. date: 09/16/2016

To order additional copies of this book, contact:
Xlibris
800-056-3182
www.Xlibrispublishing.co.uk
Orders@Xlibrispublishing.co.uk
735251

CONTENTS

Acknowledgements ix

How To Use This Book xi

Introduction xiii

My Journey xv

Section 1. Understanding Your Spacecraft 1

    Driving Your Vehicle—What Is in Control? 2

    Your Spacecraft 4

    How Much Are You Worth? 5

    We Are Running on Autopilot. 7

    The Voices in Our Heads 10

    Who Is the Pilot Today? 11

    The Fear of Change 12

    Are Your Gauges of Wealth, Happiness, and
    Success Stuck? 13

    Have You Ever Wondered Why You Don't Seem to
    be in Control? 15

    Are You Making Your Own Decisions? 17

    Do You Believe That You Can Fly? 18

    It's time for the 'What If Game' – Review Questions 20

Section 2. Some Guidelines for Flight and Maintenance 22

    Honour the Crew in Your Spacecraft. 23

    We Are Meaning Making Machines! 24

First Steps in Reprogramming Your Autopilot.................26

Be Aware! Your Fears Can Create Your Next Reality. 28

Letting Go...30

Love or Fear - Your Choice 31

What Is Disease? 33

Stuck Energy Can Move Again!................................36

Stop Beating Yourself Up! 38

Failure or Another Disguised Step Forward..................39

'No' is Almost Never Personal 41

What Are You Looking For and What Do You Notice? ...44

Improve It! Don't Attempt to Fix It! 45

Working Your Way to Heaven Won't Work! 47

Shit Happens!...49

Hold On! The Crown, the Fruit, and the Rewards
Are On Their Way!...50

It's time for the 'What If Game' – Review Questions 53

Section 3. Taking Control 55

Take Responsibility!...56

Ask How...57

What Does It Take to Become Free?...........................59

Two Things That Will Crash Your Spacecraft 61

Two Enemies of a Smooth Ride, in the Right Now........63

What do You Fill and Programme Your World With? 66

Be Careful What You Focus On! 68

Sincere Heart Cry, Can Change Your World 71

Change Is Just One Heartbeat Away . . . But?.............74

There Is an Ancient Practice That Can Change
Your World..77

No More Trying—Just Do It!..79

Why Shouldn't We? 81

The Power of Prayer..82

Choose Empowering Beliefs 84

It's Time to Take Action! But How?..................86

Take Action Anyway! 87

What Holds Us in the Darkness?.......................88

What Needs to Be Shed to Bring Us into the Light?.......89

It's time for the 'What If Game.' –
Review Questions 90

Section 4. Flying in Style...................................92

The Law of Attraction 93

Empowerment 95

What Will You Wear Today? 96

The Mystery of Money.......................................97

Have You Found Your Golden Goose?.................99

The Pursuit of Happiness 103

Sex, Nudity, Freedom, and the Divine 105

Forgiveness Is Loving Ourselves!....................107

Are You Planning Your Life? 109

Past Lives or Seeing Through the Eyes of Others
that Have Been Before? 111

Do You Desire a Soul Mate? 112

Some Tips and Ideas Experienced from My Soul
Mate Manifestation Process 114

Integrity—Live in Truth 116

I Am...118

For Those Suffering Loss 120

It's time for the 'What If Game.' –
Review Questions 122

Section 5. Fly Back to Love................................... 124

    Reaching Your Idea of Heaven Is Not the Goal—
    It's Enjoying the Journey! 125

    An Adventure in Goal Setting 127

    Have You Created a Vision Board? 130

    How Do You See the World? 132

    The Ramblings of a Mad Man 134

    Perfect Peace in the Midst of a Storm 135

    The Tapestry of Life 137

    The Mystery of the Temples and Life 140

    Death – The Ultimate Journey 142

    Void, Nothingness, or a Place of Loving Energy? 144

    You Never Lose by Giving 145

    All You Need Is Love 148

    Where Are You Choosing to Live? 150

    It's Time for the 'What If Game.' – Review Questions... 153

In Conclusion 155

Appendix 157

#KeyWords 157

Index 187

Recommended Books, Audio Programmes, Mentors,
and Movies 197

About the Author 201

ACKNOWLEDGEMENTS

In gratitude, I stand on the shoulders of giants. Those that have gone before—their learnings and wisdom passed down throughout the ages and generations, through great leaders, prophets, teachers, authors and storytellers and onwards in time, finally reaching us. I believe it is a part of our destiny to live and refine those truths for our modern age and then to pass them on.

I have benefitted and have learned from so many. It would be difficult to name all the influencers—from the hundreds of books I have read; audiotapes listened to, videos watched, and courses, workshops and webinars attended. You will see many of them mentioned throughout the book and especially in the 'My Journey' section.

I would especially like to thank my parents, past wives and my children for the moments of joy, connection and Love. Also for the tough moments, lessons, and growth created from so many interactions. It is the hard times and the failures that also make us what we are and often compound the learnings Life has for us.

All these experiences have been drawn on and helped produce the beliefs and insights shared in this book. Sometimes too it can be the dandy bad examples we have seen or been, that help us to grow!

Acknowledgements

So first I'd like to thank Life and Spirit for all the Love and beauty brought, and also for the wisdom that has been produced through the times of Life's fascinating anvil and purging fires.

I'd especially like to thank Rose O'Mahony for her dedication, questions and helping ideas that have flowed into some of the topics covered, and our funny agreements and disagreements on the punctuation. Also Alison Jones from *Tell Your Story* for some ideas shared and tweaks to the content, and finally, the team at Xlibris for their work on the final production and publication.

HOW TO USE THIS BOOK

Feel free to read it straight through or browse at will. This is a manual and guidebook for life's journey, and like any manual or guidebook there will be ideas you are already familiar with – lessons you have learned. So please feel free to skip around and browse for the posts which most appeal to you. Rather than the conventional chapters of a novel, this book is arranged in sections and individual posts or topics. Each topic is complete in itself, and the sections follow a general flow and path.

You may also choose to use the index and #Keywords lists. (The #KeyWords list covers the main subjects of each particular topic/post, whereas the Index includes many of the words used in the text.) These can help you follow a path through areas that are of particular interest, or where you are currently opening to growth. Maybe at times you can just set an intention and flip open a page to see where Spirit will take you.

It often seems that with further reading, the contents of books have changed over time. However, it is just as we grow, that deeper lessons continue to unfold. So come back to the book from time to time and see what speaks to you then. Continual learning keeps us growing and alive!

At the end of each section are some questions from the 'What If Game.' This game gives you the chance to dream and explore the possibilities and outcomes that may arise when you answer its questions. It can prompt ideas and answers and help visualise what may happen if you follow a particular path or make different choices—all without risk. If you like, listen to the answers that come, and where these questions and thoughts lead. You may then want to explore, make any changes or build affirmations and actions to create and manifest these new realities.

Once upon a time, we all played games. Then they were real to us! After that, someone said, we had to grow up!

Even rereading some of the areas that seem basic can often uncover deeper insights and paint our understanding in richer colours.

I look forward to sharing this journey with you.

INTRODUCTION

Did you realise we are flying on our journey here in an amazing spacecraft? We land here on this earth, in our body, a spacecraft perfectly fit for our survival here. Initially, we don't have a clue about who or what we are. By the time understanding is starting to form, our thought patterns, reactions, and habits have already been programmed by others—our DNA, our parents, our religions, our schools, the media, and so many other external influences. Many of these thought patterns are frequently compounded by the often-flawed decisions, and the meanings we have made about events we have experienced. To top it off, when we start to wake up, we discover there is no user manual or guidebook to help us on our journey, and we don't even know whom we can trust to ask questions along the way.

The following lessons, messages, and thoughts are ideas and tips that have been accumulated in my life—a journey full of experiences, and a study of some of the wise souls and thought leaders who have featured in my growth. It has got to a point where all the wisdom I have accumulated has to come bubbling out from a wellspring of spirit deep within. I'd like to share some of this with you in the hope that even a few of the words, learnings, and ideas can become a source of direction, inspiration, and guidance. Join me as we 'Fly Back to Love' together.

Following are some more details and a brief story of my life to help you understand my journey. If you'd rather, feel free to skip this and proceed to the first chapter 'Understanding Your Spacecraft.'

MY JOURNEY

Before we go off exploring our spacecrafts, may I begin by sharing some of my journey and history?

I was born in the early '50s, to what originally was quite a poor, young, newlywed couple. My father was ambitious and was driven to achieve. He studied, worked hard, and rose in success.

I inherited much of his drive, although I also knew where I didn't want to go. It seemed like I was a great disappointment to him, failing my 11 plus exam and not wanting to endure all the years of study to follow in his architect business. This resulted in being taken from a strict private school, and somewhat dumped into a local secondary school. Missing the early bonding with my peers and classmates, in a strange new school, further led to my sense of aloneness and alienation! I remember so many times lying in bed and holding my breath as long as I could, wishing I could die.

Failing rather miserably, I was lost in a time warp between two extremely different worlds. The old, a strict private school teaching Latin, French, and physics, complete with bullying and corporal punishment; and the new, a co-ed school, where the emphasis was more on the physical subjects, woodwork, geography, and technical drawing. I left with the somewhat inglorious accolade of just passing three O levels exams; maths, woodwork, and technical drawing!

I scraped into technical college where I was supposed to be studying a computer course, though ironically and hard to believe, in this changed age. At first, there wasn't even a computer in the college! We programmed on punched cards that were taken to run on a huge but very basic machine at the nearby ministry of defence building.

My studies were disrupted by newly acquired interests— becoming the social secretary of the students union. I was organising events, disk jockeying for the college radio station, and created a mobile discotheque. Even playing poker in the canteen seemed more important than creating lines of code for a distant machine.

I achieved an unverified world record for nonstop disk jockeying at that magnificent festival of all festivals—the Isle of Wight in 1970—where the gods of music, such as Jimmy Hendrix, The Who, The Moody Blues, Joan Baez, Joni Mitchell, Chicago, and many other greats played. In the middle of the night, a policeman came and told me they could hear my music on the mainland.

I don't remember much of my childhood. Many of these memories were obscured, clouded, and banished to far corners of my consciousness by the next few, rather wild years—exploring alternative universes with hash and hallucinogens and morphing into a new creature, a fully fledged hippie. I was living briefly in a commune in a nature reserve and then later, in a tent with my cat, whilst fruit picking.

I also visited one of the early Glastonbury festivals where the first pyramid stage was constructed. We were quite convinced—due to the magical nature of Glastonbury—that it would take off and fly away during the height of this incredible experience. For some of us, I think it probably did!

After another festival and a rather mind bending trip, I had forgotten who I was. A rather amazing journey of discovery ensued: I went from living in an extremely derelict building in London to working in a club in Leicester square, and then moving into a plush flat in Mayfair and playing football at Eric Clapton's house, whilst working briefly for a pop agency. This all happened in the space of about two weeks! Rags to temporary riches and then remembering and crashing back to the reality of my parent's house with severe tonsillitis. I am sure there were angels looking after me!

During these times, a deep soul hunger, with so many questions, was arising and nagging within. Who was I? What was this life about? How did 'normal' life reconcile with the many adventures in strange worlds and the consciousness I experienced? Was there a purpose to Life?

After one magical evening of soul searching and revelation, I decided my purpose must be to find and connect with God. How to do that or what God was, though, was still a complete mystery. I started my quest studying, with even greater intent, any spiritual or religious books I could find and asking questions on the way. From the Bible to the Bhagavad-Gita; from the Koran to *Was God an Astronaut?*; from the *Tibetan Book of the Dead* to the new prophets of Timothy Leary and Aldous Huxley, I devoured any glimmer of light or direction, eagerly seeking for answers.

I even spent a week in a Franciscan monastery on retreat. I ended the week sharing—in heartfelt desperation and with bitter tears—my soul's quest, frustrations, and lack of progress with a younger monk. He took me into their chapel, moved back some chairs, and taught me a beautiful yoga sequence to the Lord's Prayer. I faithfully repeated this for many days.

About nine months into my quest, many answers arrived during yet another breaking. With desperate heartfelt crying, flowing with tears of abject despondency, it seemed my world was imploding and collapsing. I picked up a Bible from the row of books on my bookshelf and it opened to Psalm 27. It seemed the very voice of God was outlining my quest, desire, and promise to find Him. The message ended with 'I had fainted unless I had believed to see the goodness of the Lord in the land of the living. Wait on the Lord, be of good courage and he shall strengthen thy heart.'

Deep inside, I knew I had been heard and answers were coming! A few days later, I met some wonderful people at another festival; they were feeding, singing, and helping those in need. I recognised the call to join them and after a night of deep soul searching, I realised I had a big choice: I could live my life for me, carrying on how I wanted, or I could follow Spirit, giving my life and all to help others.

This calling led to twenty years of rather radical, somewhat fanatical, unconventional Christian-based voluntary work all over the world, living mainly in communities. I worked in the UK, Holland, France, Peru, the Dominican Republic, India, Sri Lanka, and Poland.

Years later, my children no longer fitted in with this international travelling and community lifestyle. As young teens, they had their own worlds and lives to explore. Sadly, I had to leave and there was a new life to carve out.

During the later times in this voluntary work, I had been asking companies to donate computers and then training others to use them. Now I was led to use these skills and contacts. In life, it seems there is always some direction and guidance. I believe all the things we go through and learn have an accumulated purpose as our lives unfold.

After a start-up business course, I was beginning again from scratch with nothing to invest. I bought and then sold a second-hand computer; buying two, selling them; buying four, selling them; onwards and upwards it went. Some years later, I reached the goal of a million pounds turnover. It seemed Spirit had blessed me and everything I had given up in the twenty years before was multiplied and given back—a beautiful mansion in the countryside with large beautiful grounds, a tennis court and pool, a new relationship, and new friends.

Yet soon, I watched this crash and burn. I had been working for the worst boss of all, a real slave driver, who had forgotten many of the values he should have held dear—Me! The computer industry changed drastically, the big boys spoilt the field, cutting out the little people in their drive to dominate; and the Internet took over, cutting prices and making the best deals available to all at the click of a mouse.

Fortunately, I had bolted on a little part time business, born originally from a desire to help my customers. Initially, I hadn't realised how this seemingly insignificant step and small extra income source could change my life. Soon I began to realise what an amazing opportunity it was. As Jim Rohn said, I was finding myself 'working full time on my business and part time on my fortune'. I had discovered a golden goose that initially lay pretty small but regular eggs, and they were soon growing monthly.

The computer business crashed and bankruptcy loomed, I was cutting every extra to the bone. Even a few of life's seeming necessities were sacrificed. Fortunately, the growing income from that network marketing business saved the day! Now, some years later, it pays more than my bills every month and is enough to also cover many holidays. One of my passions is exploring the world. I also have the pleasure of sitting here writing, without the constraints and commitments of a full time job. Besides, I am completely unemployable.

After years of freedom, I don't think I could handle any boss controlling my every minute ever again!

That business turned out to be a personal development organisation in disguise. Much of the emphasis to achieve success was in training and personal growth. One of my earliest mentors suggested that I study the wisdom of Jim Rohn. The challenge to 'Become the person that success can find, rather than hunting down success', started me again on a path of discovery and personal growth. I attended, in spite of very limited funds, what turned out to be his last public weekend in Dallas, before his terminal illness. I am so glad I made that effort! Sometimes you have to follow where Spirit leads, no matter what the cost!

His wise words and those of other teachers led me to define my purpose; 'To Love, to Learn, to Teach', and I later added, 'to Enjoy Success'. I decided one of my goals would be to sit at the feet of masters and learn from them. It has now become my vision to pass the wisdom and the learnings I have gained onto the world. This and the desire to support and teach, has led me to spend, as Jim suggested, 'more on feeding my mind than just on feeding my body.'

I have grown from classes with Jim Rohn, Bob Proctor, Brian Tracy, Robert Kiyosaki, and many others. I have spent hours listening to or reading the words of Earl Nightingale, Napoleon Hill, Wayne Dyer, Wallace Wattles, Neale Donald Walsch, and many other leaders of thought and Spirituality. I studied in workshops with Tony Robbins, Clinton Swayne, Harv T. Eker, Christopher Howard, Les Brown, and many others. The Secret and its teachers have filled me and answered many of my questions. The Law of Attraction, Quantum Physics, NLP and many ideas and teachings have permeated throughout my being, filling with understanding.

I also experienced the collapse of my second marriage and embarked on a journey of soul searching, soul mate seeking, and understanding relationships with Arielle Ford, John Gray, and other great teachers. Starting dating again, after eighteen years of marriage, I've had the blessing of manifesting my desire for a new soul mate. I have studied many courses in personal development, NLP, hypnotism, health and healing, tantra and wealth creation. So many lessons learned that now, these things are bubbling over and pouring out. I discovered a still, small voice within that takes the many truths from these things, and seems to bring out the best and most appropriate, when needed.

Now as a result of this lifetime of growth and experience, I'd like to share with you some of the learning's and thoughts from my journey, in the hope that even just a few of these ideas can provide some help, maybe a little wisdom and some guidance. They could be signposts of potential ways forward if you ever feel stuck on your voyage through this world. I hope and trust that some will prove useful in reconnecting you with Love, and on your voyage back to the Source. That Source which is the amazing energy, which I choose to believe in and call Love.

SECTION 1

Understanding Your Spacecraft

'We are not human beings in search of a spiritual experience. We are spiritual beings immersed in a human experience.' –Wayne W. Dyer

Now before we fly off in earnest, I must share an important point with you. The things I am about to share are not ultimate truths and in fact, for you, may or may not be true or false. For me, they are my truths and many empowering beliefs that are honed, and are working well on my journey. Please weigh each of them in the centre of your own heart. If they feel true and work for you, then please feel free to adopt those that work; if not, I am sure you can find and embrace your own truths, those that will inspire and speed your journey. I don't feel there are any ultimate blacks and whites; rather, just beautifully coloured worlds for us to explore and enjoy on our voyages here.

Driving Your Vehicle—What Is in Control?

'If you correct your mind, the rest of your life will fall into place.' – Lao Tzu.

How would it feel if the vehicle you were driving suddenly developed a mind of its own and turned in many opposite directions and down roads that you weren't choosing? Driven by an autopilot, mostly out of your control.

Would you sit patiently and watch?

Would you attempt to wrest back control?

Would you see if you could jump out?

Would you struggle for a while and then eventually give up, and just fall asleep in frustration and despair?

Or, maybe you'd slam on the brakes, search for the manual, or find help to get it fixed?

To wake up in what is an amazing organic spacecraft, realising there is little or very limited control and no manual—this can be very frustrating and a frightening experience, which could be why many people are content to drift on in whatever direction the craft is heading.

This amazing craft, five trillion living parts, working in community as one! It's a powerhouse of energy, light, and life! There are thousands of separate systems and controls. They are, in most cases, working well together and for the greater good of the entire body.

Waking from some kind of hyper-sleep state drifting in and out of consciousness, I discovered that some of the systems, especially guidance and direction, have been hijacked and reprogrammed by others, rather than by the maker. Some of the gauges have also got stuck in flight, limiting levels of happiness, wealth, and success. These are often set at far different levels than I would like.

Your Spacecraft

'We may not be responsible for the world that created our minds, but we can take responsibility for the mind with which we create our world.' – Gabor Maté

Your Spacecraft is a most wonderful craft. Trillions of individual cells are working together, creating the most amazing machine known to man.

Strangely though, most people seem to believe we are the spacecraft; but we are not the spacecraft! We are just voyaging here on a temporary journey in this spacecraft.

Similarly, we are not all the voices we hear in our heads. Most of humanity hears these same voices. Many of these voices are beliefs and fears that have been floating around, in different languages or forms for thousands of years!

They are all a part of our autopilot programming. Some are from our ancestors, some from our parents, some from our religions, and some from our schooling. Yes, we have filtered these beliefs and, in many cases, added our own interpretations to them. These have, for lots of people, made the jumble of noise, fears, and opinions that are running their lives almost unbearable. No wonder decision-making can prove difficult, and many of us attempt to avoid it!

To grow, it is now time to clear out the clutter, take control of our spacecraft, and reprogramme it with our own empowering beliefs.

How Much Are You Worth?

'It is not what you say out of your mouth that determines your life, it's what you whisper to yourself that has the most power.' – Robert Kiyosaki

Your spacecraft actually has huge value. If it could be valued for all the chemicals, minerals, and even gold inside, you would find a surprisingly large answer, and that's without the huge amounts of energy generated in a lifetime, its pumping systems, and other resources.

However, the most important question is: How much do you think *you* are worth? It is all about your self-worth! Many of us, earth voyagers, when just a short time into the beginning of our voyages, decided that as our parents were perfect, anything that went wrong had to be our fault. Others succumbed to bullying, whether in school or by more subtle pressures. Sometimes, even well-meaning parents whose methods of child raising and discipline were often limited to harsh attention of every little failing, followed by showers of scorn and a big *you* did it wrong, *you* are useless. This was often followed up with so many 'no's that a simple 'no' becomes a barrier that many of us fear to cross. Even if they didn't say it so directly, many of us decided these, or many of our other experiences or childhood incidents, meant that we were completely useless and doomed to failure.

The voices in our heads and our self-talk have taken up the crusade of this demeaning rubbish, which has been pouring through our beings for so long. For many, listening to this negative mind chatter has become a lifelong habit! The poor creature that is piloting our crafts has often now shrivelled almost into non-existence, a being despising itself.

Imagine if someone broke into your home and started yelling at you or your children in this manner! You would have them arrested or, at the very least, throw them out. Yet, most of us

5

have tolerated similar voices in our heads for years, with their insidious lies that have slowly been destroying our joy and the possibility of our successes. In so many of our endeavours, these voices have been stealing so much of our power!

Is it time to throw off the old habits and create new empowering voices in our heads, cheering us on, as we voyage here?

We Are Running on Autopilot.

'First we form habits, then they form us. Conquer your bad habits or they will conquer you.' – Rob Gilbert

A friend and mentor of mine, Big Al, Tom Schreiter, posed an interesting task: Ask one hundred people how they make a decision?

The results can be rather scary, as most people have no idea! This is an especially challenging realisation if you are in the business of helping people make decisions!

The conscious mind is only capable of handling one thought at a time. This leaves the incredibly complex and wonderful, subconscious, mind running our spacecraft the rest of the time. How does it do it? With a series of learned tasks and habits, these programmes are running on our autopilot. They control every action and automatically make almost every decision. Scientists tell us it is often done, even before the conscious mind kicks in and realises; there are even questions, or a task at hand.

Now this is a good thing most of the time! Imagine how it would be if you had to make a conscious decision about everything. You would barely be out of bed in the morning before the day was over, and too tired to do anything else but go back to sleep!

The thinking and decision process begins. Shall I wake up now? Which muscle shall I use first to open my eyes? Oh, two eyes at once, those are a lot more muscles, and they all have to be fired in the right sequence! Then along comes the task of firing and coordinating most of the muscles in the body. That's just for the 'simple' task of sitting up and getting out of bed. I know, I have had a painful back for the last couple of days and it's been an incredible education in what parts of my body move during various tasks, and the muscles have been

7

shooting pains of protest, even when performing the simplest of actions! My, how much we take for granted!

Now begins the processes of the day, a trip to the bathroom, washing or showering, brushing teeth, etc. Take a moment to consider how many commands were involved in actioning and coordinating even one of the simple activities that we take so much for granted! I wonder if you are anything like me. Something can happen to upset the normal sequence of events, and later I could realise an important action had been forgotten, such as shaving before rushing out of the door!

It sure makes me grateful that I don't have to consider and consciously run every moment of the show! However then, the thought must come to mind: who and what programmed my most of important actions and decisions? It seems many of these were programmed years ago at different age when I wasn't wise enough or capable of making my own choices. Many have been instilled by parents or by schooling. Some even programmed long before by the genetic survival responses buried deep in some ancestors past.

Many of these automatic programmes use the power of fear to enforce their authority.

Now, many programmes are still beneficial, but let's search out and consider some that are no longer useful and may hinder our current progress and plans. Yet in many of us, they can still be running in the background.

As a little child, 'Don't talk to strangers' was a wise and helpful programme. However, the subconscious fears invoked, and the reluctance to risk disobeying these deep down feelings can become a major hindrance. Imagine that programme running later in a job or situation, when meeting others has become a vital task for success. Now many people have successfully realised this and reprogrammed. For others, that little whispering fear and the seeming disobedience to their gut feelings of safety has become a hindrance to their social lives and business successes.

Many parents, too, have ingrained the belief that 'You can't have everything you want!' They were probably hoping to allay disappointments, or maybe excuse their inability to provide. However, if that program continues running in later life, it can kill any dream and provide a quick excuse for giving up on expecting your very best.

Would it be okay to take some time to think of and catalogue how many of these old programmes could be hindering your current progress and success?

Is it time to reprogramme your autopilot?

The Voices in Our Heads

'If you realised how powerful thoughts are, you'd never think a negative thought again.' – Peace Pilgrim

'What voices?' I hear you say, 'I don't hear voices!' Consider for a moment that that could have been one of those many voices. Are these voices or thoughts all ours? Identifying with them too closely or following the most extreme can be a dangerous business. Where are they taking you? Do they have a mind of their own? It is time to stand back and become the observer and examine each one. Will it take you where you'd like to go? Is it worth checking out to see what kind of fruit it could grow? Would following it hasten an already downward spiral, speeding to a future railroad crash; or could it lift up, strengthen, inspire, and move you onwards and upwards towards your desires and dreams?

No, you can't choose all your thoughts, but you can choose to stop the ones you don't like from nesting in your hair! Shoo them off like you would pigeons coming to eat the newly growing seeds in your garden. Then build a net of belief, over those freshly growing shoots to protect them from any past habitual fat birds that would seek to devour them and you.

Who Is the Pilot Today?

'Until you make the unconscious conscious, it will control your life and you will call it fate.'—Carl Jung

As well as there being different personality types of people, I am more and more convinced that at different times, we each have within us different personalities or archetypes piloting our spacecraft. Sometimes, there is even a battle going on about who will take the controls. In some extremes, there are times when the personality divide is so strong that one part of a person's being doesn't know what the other part is doing and each can have completely different physical symptoms and characteristics.

Step into the observer role for a while and think about the times when your inner child has come to help you be playful, or a more spoilt version, thrown a fit. Maybe your controller has taken over to help stabilise things or attempts to take over a situation with others. Or, maybe your sensual lover, goddess, or king, has shown up for a night of passion. We can each step into roles for different tasks or experiences. Or, are these experiences actually part of a greater us, there to help us; or sometimes, if we yield to them, more impetuous spirits causing grief?

The Fear of Change

'Change can be scary, but you know what's scarier? Allowing fear to stop you from growing, evolving and progressing!' — *Mandy Hale*

Our decision-making processes and the ability to make the changes that we desire are frequently hindered by subconscious fears that were implanted long before. Sometimes, when we have been burnt by previous bad experiences, these residual fears now hinder and stop, or slow us down from taking the brave steps forward into new worlds of success and growth.

Ever shrinking comfort zones can lead to lives filled with mediocrity, routine, and early graves. We are often chained like the eagle that had been attached to a stake so long that now, even though freed and the chain long gone, he still keeps pacing the old ruts. His once magnificent life, soaring through mountains and nature, when previously free, is long forgotten– just a distant memory of a destiny that could have been.

Yet for us, there is still the chance to throw off the chains of fear and conformity–to write our own programmes. We can start living once again the empowered life that is our birthright and destiny.

Do you desire it enough, to take the steps, to make it happen?

Are Your Gauges of Wealth, Happiness, and Success Stuck?

'You can have anything you want, if you are willing to give up the belief that you can't have it.' – Robert Anthony

Our levels of fuels, drivers, and comforts for our voyage, often seem to be stuck or set at levels far below what would seem good or what we deeply desire. They are often pre-programmed by limiting beliefs and accepted norms and ideas. So we are, in fact, stuck exactly where our beliefs hold us.

Conformity to our social classes used to be an incredibly strong bond, which now is losing its control in many societies. Maybe it is the seeds of ideas sown by our parents or peers that result in us being uncomfortable with not fitting in; or is it fears of jealousy of friends or siblings?

Is it deep down feelings of unworthiness, untold fears of failures, or even fears of success and all the changes they may bring? Those are just some of the things that hold people back. How about *you*? If you get really quiet, take a couple of deep breaths, still the ego, and listen to your beautiful heart. What would it share?

What if, for a few moments, you took some time and gave yourself permission to dream; what would you desire?

Did you know that if you really and I mean, *really,* want those things, you can have them? Now, it may take a bit of work especially in rearranging your beliefs and the running auto programmes. This is because, on some level, I believe we are currently receiving and living exactly what we have desired or pre-programmed, even those stuck levels to accept. It is the programmes we are running that disempower us, not some limits in our reality!

Maybe in the past, it was a secret desire for conformity, a feeling of unworthiness, or the need for penance, and the secret shames of being different that held you back? Are you ready to shed past fears and limitations and take full control of your direction again?

It is time to fill up with *love*, pour on some deep abiding *joy*, and let loose some extra *happiness*, without the worry about those who would consider you insane! Let's rip out all thoughts of conformity and fly. The fulfilment of your desires and intentions is just around the corner from abandoned old beliefs and habits.

Have You Ever Wondered Why You Don't Seem to be in Control?

'I hold three treasures close to my heart. The first is love; the next, simplicity; the third, overcoming ego.' —Tao Te Ching

Or even what, or who you are?

Just like our body is comprised of trillions of cells working together in community, and millions of these cells form together–for like functions–creating amongst other things our vital organs, I believe, we are also made up of many personalities. These personas, especially the ones controlling our personalities, each have vital roles to play in different activities and times in our lives. All of these too, can become like or almost run as automatic responses or programmes, with what appears to be minds of their own.

Some programmes that help run us are more basic background controls, running the automatic functions of our bodies; and others can be almost like people, personalities in their own rights, taking over control of our interactions and reactions as we journey through our lives. Examples of these parts could be the inner child, the mother, the goddess, the lover, the controller, the father, etc.

Life has given us many tools and programmes for our journey here. I choose the belief that all of these are for our basic good, though maybe some are left over from different ages or times in our lives.

One of the main parts of our ancient brain is the system that fires chemicals throughout our cells for protection to help us react quickly to danger. This automatic response is our fight or flight mode kicking in. Unfortunately, this often now keeps us in our new human environment, permanently dosed with stress chemicals, unless we tame that response with meditation, rest, or other calming, relaxing, stress releasing tools.

15

Another persona or programme at times running, or let's say crewing our earthly spacecraft, could be our inner child. Sometimes, this child has been programmed by abusive parents, or a draconian education system, or fear of reprisals by a hell-wielding religion. So it can be that the inner child comes out to play or wreak havoc by throwing its fits.

Then there is the ego, often considered as the worst enemy of spirituality, demanding to be heard above all, shouting its instructions about the way it expects to control our craft.

I am sure you can identify many other crew or archetypes in your spaceship. They often come to the forefront and demand that they fly the craft their way, and choose the direction of your flight.

Even as adults ourselves, it's quite frequent that we suddenly automatically revert to patterns and programmes observed in childhood, from our parents, and act or become like our mother or our father. This can be great if they were good role models; however, it is often the bad habits we copy. Have you ever had the thought 'I'm turning out just like my parents?'

Too often, all these different parts and programmes are vying for attention and the controls. They end up filling our minds with so much chatter and confusion that it can become difficult to make decisions, or hear the flight instructions from mission control, let alone be your own person! Or maybe one strong crewman has taken control, not realising that it only sees its own limited picture of its role in the journey.

Now all these parts—especially the meeker, quieter ones— have an important role in our journey through life. However, some have accepted the wrong information and programming. I know deep inside, after all the confusion is removed, each part has its own important role to play. When drilled down to the very basic core of their desire, each part is designed, and seeks the greater good of the whole craft.

Are You Making Your Own Decisions?

'Your thoughts affect your emotions. Your emotions affect your decisions. Your decisions affect your life.' – Author Unknown

Whatever happens on your flight, one of the things all pilots do is calmly assessing each situation and deciding what they feel about it, how it affects them, what level of danger it could pose, and all the other what ifs. They then choose the appropriate actions they can take.

As they say, 'our attitude affects our altitude'. How high would you like to fly? How about if you stood between the vision or experience of each event and your automatic preprogrammed reactions—and *paused*? What if you had the ultimate power to breathe a deep breath and consider how you would like to react or change course, before charging headfirst into some unknown or negative situation?

I know as flight commanders, we have that ability! It may just take a while to find and learn how to use that control. Also, to use some practice in its implementation and direction. However, the ultimate choice and responsibility is given to us, in how we control and fly our craft. It's time to seize control back from the autopilot and the programmes of others, and fly back to love! You are the pilot! You have the *power*! Seize the day!

Do You Believe That You Can Fly?

'It's impossible to live without failing at something, unless you live so cautiously that you might as well not have lived at all. In which case, you've failed by default.' – J. K. Rowling

Too many pilots have lost the confidence to fly. A one-time crash, or a flight instructor's demeaning attitude has left them with the belief that taking off again is just not for them. Goals and dreams have been abandoned either forever, or put on long-term hold, because of the realisation that it would take a flight to reach them. Deep down there is a nagging fear of failure. This leaves too many potentially great pilots working as ground crew, having lost, or maybe never found the belief that they could fly.

The trouble is, you are in a spacecraft that is designed to fly high, and you are stuck on the ground. If you are still afraid to take the controls, or running on autopilot and just coasting above the ground, then it's going to be a pretty uneventful and miserable ride through life.

Failed self-confidence, knocks, and crashes—or the programming that you are just not good enough—has left too many of us afraid to dream mainly because of fears, or for 'protection' from further failures.

In worst cases, some people can even be afraid to step out of their houses. For many folks, it has become close to difficult—or verging on impossible—to make any kind of changes or decisions. Whether it's an unsatisfying job, a failed relationship, or just stretching to make that dream holiday happen, it becomes too easy to rest in mediocrity. Numerous fears can hold us captive and firmly on the ground in a rusting spacecraft that was once designed to fly.

Never fear though, as it is always possible to get the craft flying again! Write some new programmes, replace the fuel, and take off towards your destiny. We are designed to fly high! It just takes some adjustment of that autopilot, refuelling with good, clean and fresh fuel, a bit of retraining, and we can all be on our exciting flight back to *Love* and loving every moment.

The majesty of choice is ours! I firmly believe there is no dream that can enter the heart of man, without Spirit or Love, also being able to make a way to help us fulfil it. We only have to do our part and make those first steps in preparing our craft, waiting for that first surge of power, and then following the directions from our ultimate guidance systems. Homing beacons and mission control can then help us through the route and to fly onwards to the destiny of our choice.

Self-confidence, Self-love, Belief, and Faith are some of the steps to flying again. We will cover how to find and grow these in the next chapters.

It's time for the 'What If Game' – Review Questions

The 'What If Game' is a great opportunity to explore any ideas, plans, and directions. This is without fear, or the idea that you have to follow any of the answers provided by your ever-eager imagination. Let that imagination flow and consider a few scenarios, a bit like brainstorming. Then choose any answers or plans that you especially like. After all, with 'What If,' they are only possibilities and you can still decide if you'd like to further pursue any of your discovered answers. One of life's important skills is learning how to ask great questions!

You can make up your own 'What If' questions too. It's simple—just think of any appropriate questions that fit the ideas and possibilities you'd like to explore, add a 'What If,' and then take a while—if possible in a quiet place—to think and listen for answers and directions. It is amazing how our subconscious mind loves to bring us answers to the questions we pose. It just takes us listening for them—with an open mind—and not being afraid to ask!

Okay? Let's go! Now the magic of manifestation can begin.

What if any of my fears could be exposed and leave—which would I choose?

What if I was suddenly free of fear—what would I choose to do?

What if I could clearly see my autopilot and habitual programmes?

What if I suddenly had a clear vision of my limiting beliefs—what is holding me back?

What if there was one area in my life that a magic wand could change—which would I choose?

What if a secret desire could be guaranteed fulfilled—which would I choose?

What if I knew deep inside that I was an indestructible being with the majesty of choice—how would I live?

SECTION 2

Some Guidelines for Flight and Maintenance

Honour the Crew in Your Spacecraft.

'Teamwork: Coming together is a beginning, keeping together is progress, working together is success.' – Henry Ford

I once heard someone say that the ego must be destroyed. At times, I feel sure each of us has tried to suppress some of the different parts and personas that appear to be crying out or taking control within us.

It's time to stop any mutinies and help each part of us to realise they are just a crewmember. Yes, they have a vital role, but unless they appreciate and return to their place, they could risk the success of the entire mission. They too must be honoured, and learn to honour all the other crewmembers on the mission and appreciate each of other's vital roles.

Remembering our true state as spiritual beings on an earthly journey, could it be time to identify and get back to the centre? Surely it's time to assume your true role as the commander of your spacecraft! Take the time to rein in any domineering thought patterns or crewmembers, whose single-minded determination could threaten the whole craft. Let's remember to honour each one for their place, and help all the parts of us to fulfil their true purpose and ultimate desire, which is to help the craft fly smoothly and in unison back to *love*.

If you would like to spend some time with a truly funny view of this beautiful parallel, search out and watch the movie 'Meet Dave' with Eddie Murphy.

We Are Meaning Making Machines!

'Life is without meaning. You bring the meaning to it. The meaning of life is whatever you ascribe it to be. Being alive is the meaning.' – Joseph Campbell

Whenever anything happens to us, thoughts usually come up and go into activity to search for a meaning or reason; and also, often to look for where to place the blame. Do everything you can to avoid placing blame! Taking personal responsibility for every event is one of the first steps to finding new directions and flying back to *Love*.

Now this human characteristic of making meanings can be positive. That is, if we are attuned to great basic beliefs, such as: 'Life Loves Me', 'All things work together for good', 'There is no such thing as failure'. Sadly, however, many of us have picked up the habit of allowing negative belief patterns and emotions to come to the forefront of our thinking, and then due to the constant flood of these thoughts and ideas, letting them influence our journeys and moods, frequently dragging us down.

It is amazing how many different meanings can be placed on every situation that occurs. Just like when a policeman interviews different witnesses to an accident, each one has a different perspective of what happened and a different story of where the blame lies.

I wonder how would our lives change if we constantly sought for the good in all of the situations and events that befall us?

It is amazing looking back at my life how some events that seemed like disasters at the time have, in reality, proved over time to be blessings in disguise. The loss of a job set me free. The failure of a business again set me free from working most of the hours in each day and almost every day of the year. It gave me the opportunity to live a new and far more balanced life, thus finally attaining a far healthier life-work balance. (Yes, who said this should be the other way around?) Now, I'm able and learning to take the time to enjoy and live my life more fully.

I am convinced that serious illnesses or even deaths surely have their places in the bigger plans of life. Yes, at the time these seemingly tragic events are hard to understand or accept, but if we could just view them from the spirit and the perspective of eternity, I am sure we would then understand, and probably realise, that the greater 'Us' had planned them all along.

Let's set a guard over the meanings we make and then accept. Let's see, even if it's tough, that we can find the place to believe that 'Life Loves Us' and everything that happens is unfolding in perfection. These beliefs sure make for a less ruffled, more confident and peaceful journey.

Pause to consider: How is your journey going? How could a change of meanings and beliefs benefit and make life more meaningful, and help create a path to all you desire?

First Steps in Reprogramming Your Autopilot

'Life is not about waiting for storms to pass. It's about learning to dance in the rain.' –Author Unknown

Much of our programming is held in the form of deep-rooted ideas and beliefs. These beliefs then automatically come to mind and run our autopilot. Some event or interaction occurs, and these little programmes run and control our feelings and their meanings, and thus, also the choices, decisions and actions taken about the events that we encounter each day.

Here are two main ways we can take back control and run programmes that we choose. They work best hand in hand, used together.

1. Mindfulness.

Learn how to be in the state of being mindful. Be the observer of all you experience, then stand between the thoughts that come about the event and your choice of the meaning, and any decisions and actions you take. Realise that each thought is just another voice or possibility floating through your being. It's not yours, until you claim it, own it, and decide to act on it! Or you can choose to just let it float on meaninglessly by. There will be plenty of other thoughts coming by soon! Maybe with better cultivation, intention, affirmation and practice, many more of these flowing thoughts will be in line with your chosen directions.

2. Programme your thought patterns and the chatter in your head.

One of my early mentors shared a great method of programming he used to train his thoughts and beliefs. This was a great tool that I also used successfully in the beginning of my quest to take greater control of my thoughts, and thus the direction of my spacecraft.

When reading, he wrote down every quote that stood out and spoke to him, on a series of cards. Each day, first thing in the morning, several times thorough the day, and then last thing at night he would review and even memorise these quotes. They say it takes about 30 days for the things we do to become habits and a part of our reality.

I even eventually recorded my quotes and listened to them many times. I know they helped me take new directions in my life and became a part of my programming, beliefs, and thus frequent thoughts.

Interestingly, a couple of the pertinent quotes that I adopted were statements of the belief that the way to control my life was to take control of my thoughts. Though at that time, I had no idea of how to accomplish that intention. That practice was in effect starting to take control and help make it so.

Give it a go! I am sure following that idea and similar practices with affirmations can help reprogramme your thoughts too. Persistence, over time, pays off!

Be Aware! Your Fears Can Create Your Next Reality.

'Every thought we think is creating our future.' – Louise Hay

The crazy thing is that almost none of the fears we experience are real, or will ever come to pass! Thoughts, if repeated enough, will tend to become the realities of the imagination in which we dwell.

If this were even remotely possible, what would you do? What would you choose to think? What would you choose to believe? Can you find the power to say 'shoo, shoo' to the dark birds of fear that seek to land in your world, that way they will fly on harmlessly by? They are just dark clouds, blown swiftly and sent on their way by the ever-blowing winds of change.

Know that between the clouds, and always above the clouds, the sun ever shines. Even during the worst and darkest night of the soul, the sun is just on the other side of your planet, speeding towards a new sunrise. A fresh, purified, and rested you will soon be welcoming a new day!

Make a list of some of your common fears and then one by one, for each, ask yourself these questions. It could help to also work out which are the real fears and which are the imaginary ones.

Can you consider there is even a small possibility this is real?

Is there a chance that you could let go of this fear?

Have other people let go of similar fears and conquered them?

If you could, would you like to let go of this fear?

When would you like to let go of this fear?

Would you like to let go of this fear now?

Can you envision it as being just a dark bird flying away?

If you'd like, pin your fear on that dark bird and watch it fly away.

If you like, give yourself permission to let go. You can let go now!

After all which would you really prefer: a life full of the manifestations of your fears; or if you could, would you rather choose a life painted with the bright colours, heavenly sounds, and the ecstatic feelings of your choice?

Take some time now to dream, visualise, and create a story full of the feelings of, and the outcomes, that you would really like. This could be as simple as imagining a result in the mail, a response from a test, the reaction of a friend, the success of a whole project, or the beginning of a new relationship.

Yes, you could be right. None of this is real, and maybe it won't completely change every situation; but, if there was even a small possibility it would, could it be worth it?

I think it was Mark Twain that said, 'I have had a thousand fears and most of them never arrived.'

Hang in there; there is always a rainbow to be found after a storm, and in the belief 'Life Loves Me.'

Letting Go

'The Sedona Method stands head and shoulders above any other self-improvement technique I've ever seen.' – Jack Canfield

The questions I shared in the last post were based on the Sedona Method. It is a very powerful tool that can be used to help you or others 'Let Go' of anything that is bothering, hindering, or no longer wanted in your *life*. When you remove your internal blocks, it is amazing how *life* can let you fly!

This method has had considerable results and many great teachers use it, or variations of it, to help or heal themselves and others. It is all about choices and using the power of our conscious and unconscious minds to give ourselves permission, to realise that whatever we may choose to give up is a possibility, and then move on to actually letting go of it, if that is our choice.

I believe we are all blessed with the power of choice and when we believe this, 'All things are possible.' Sometimes though, when we get stuck in our ruts, it is difficult to see above them. The ruts of fear and stuck programming have often created deep pits where a helping hand or permission to rise above the mire of life's problems can be a great help. This can be all it takes to be propelled out of those ruts and overcome.

If you hold a pencil in your hand, then you open your hand, let go, and then turn your hand upside down, the pencil will fall out. So it is with our issues when we open our beliefs, choose, and let go of any that no longer empower us. With the right tools and practices, they can be gone!

If this resonates, I would suggest reading the book '*The Sedona Method*' by Hale Dwoskin, or taking one of their courses. There is a lot more detail covered there, and lots of ways shared that will help you to successfully use this powerful method.

Love or Fear - Your Choice

'Love or Fear, the decision defines you.' —Oprah Winfrey

There exist only two states: *Love* or *fear*. When we can stand as an observer, take a deep breath of clarity and see which of these realms the thoughts that are bombarding our consciousness are emanating from, then we have the power to accept and embrace, or let them go, and shun them.

Especially remember: you are not your thoughts! Actually, they are not *your* thoughts at all! Most of them have been flowing throughout the universe of man for many decades. Many of them are the ghosts of past troubles that have haunted mankind. You have the ability to take control and program your thoughts to be the affirmations of victories, seeking to jump into and influence your world. Love or fear: which would you like to choose?

It is a strange thing thoughts originally come like little butterflies gently wafting into our beings, and we, in innocence can easily pick them up. They can lay eggs that become like greedy caterpillars devouring the goodness in our world. They can then become beliefs and habits. The process takes time and repetition, and very soon they are like old friends, familiar and welcomed. Beware! That is, be aware! You can, too soon and too easily, get to a stage of ownership of any thoughts. – 'These are my truths, I must accept them.'

This is why, just like friends, it is so important to choose the ones that feed, uplift, and empower, rather than any which drain and pull you down to their levels. Which and who will you choose to flow with and let colour your world?

Some say, it is the age-old battle: Love versus Fear. Actually, it is all an illusion. However, it is all such a powerful illusion that in many cases, once these fears have been welcomed and accepted, they appear to take control and rule lives and even nations.

It could be as easy as choosing to face the light, rather than facing into the darkness. When we face into the light, all we can see is light and that wonderful light melts the darkness, which then flees of itself. Just believe!

Remember there is a core place within, where no matter what is happening on the outside, everything is okay. It's that magical part of you that will live forever, and cannot be touched by any of life's storms and disasters, and also, can never die!

I saw a funny, but pertinent quote today. 'We are ghosts, voyaging in meat-filled skeletons, made of stardust. So what could you possibly be afraid of?'

What Is Disease?

'True healing will always begin with your thoughts. Master your thoughts and you will master your life.' – April Peerless

We know that our outer world is created by or through the manifestation of our thoughts and feelings. As these solidify into beliefs, they create our experiences. There is also a time lag, so it is the thoughts of yesterday, which we are living in today.

It is all about the flow of these thoughts. Are they creating what we would like in our world? Disease or ill at ease comes when we are harbouring negative energy in all, or parts of our being. Instead of the negative thoughts that at times can swirl around our beings just passing through, they have been grabbed, owned, and nurtured into belief patterns, and then through habit; that negative energy can become trapped and stuck, an owned part of us, which then starts manifesting in our bodies and outer worlds.

I am convinced all of these things, like everything in our human experience, start with thought. The thoughts then create emotions, which frequently lead to words, and then deeds.

So it is habitual negative stuck energy or thoughts that lead to disease, which can manifest in so many ways, eventually ripping our peace and even our bodies apart.

Watch the thoughts in your head, unless they serve you, don't entertain them! Someone once shared with me: thoughts could become like a monkey sitting on my shoulder whispering in my ear. If kept under control and well behaved, it could be a fine pet and attraction for everyone to see. However, what if, without discipline, I let that monkey become a ferocious gorilla ranting and raving and eventually in a fit, without knowing its strength, it killed or severely hurt me?

What can we do if disease has taken over and those thoughts and energies have become a stuck ball of darkness, or growing evil reality? It is time for a miracle, transformation and change. Never fear, as there are many ways and tools to accomplish this healing. There are countless healing modalities, cures, medical procedures and miracle workers that can help.

The main thing though, it is vitally important to get to the root and make changes in the thought patterns that have created this manifesting disease in the first place. It is time to replace them with healthy, life loving, life-giving thoughts and habits.

Too often, we get stuck thinking. 'I'm tired.' 'I'm not very well.' 'I'm stressed.' 'I'm dissatisfied.' 'Nobody loves me.' 'I'm a mess,' and other similar thoughts. Even 'I'm okay,' is only a small step removed. All of these little thoughts become thought patterns and habits. Then our bodies eventually take over and live out these seemingly desired states. Those little erroneous thoughts can soon grow and wreak havoc in our world, if not controlled and sent back on their way, swirling once again through the universe. Remember if something flies by, you don't have to grab it and own it! A frequent state of dissatisfaction, those sighs of 'oh this is too much,' and other complaints about our lot in life, can also all accumulate into the weights that tie us down and hold us back.

So, Change your thoughts! Change your life! What thoughts, affirmations and actions could you incorporate into your habitual patterns that would now serve you? How would you like to feel? How about taking some regular time to think and feel that way, so that after some time, those feelings manifest and become your way of life? 'Life loves me.' 'I'm feeling great.' 'Things are getting better.' 'I am full of Loving energy.' 'I am happy, content and grateful.'

Yes gratitude is a huge key! Take time to think of what is appealing and would serve you. Now at first, there could be a little voice saying that this isn't true. So don't believe it! After all, that voice has been busy telling you its own lies for a long time! There is no lie or truth in these matters, only your thoughts and how you believe them and would like them to serve you!

Habitual thoughts can be hard to kick and their manifestations sometimes will have gone quite far, so you may need some help and time to work on them; but trust the miracle is always there. It is just waiting for the transformation of our thoughts and the growing belief that what you desire is possible.

It reminds me of a funny and very poignant skit I once saw. A psychiatrist's patient was being operated on. A crazy doctor and his monster assistant, Egor, were one by one pulling the idols of the patients mind, out of his heart. These things had been in the way of his inner peace and happiness. The fancy car, the opulent lifestyle, a stash of cocaine, several bottles of booze, a few packets of duty free cigarettes, the underwear from the dirty secret of a hidden affair, were all piled up in the corner. The patient had been sewn back up and just come round and was sharing how good he felt, when he saw the pile of his things. One by one he was grabbing them, clinging back on to them, saying how he couldn't do without each one and eventually rushing out of the operating theatre with them all in his hands again.

Egor, the assistant, asked the doctor, 'Aren't you disappointed the whole thing was a failure?' The doctor with a wry smile said, 'It's okay. When he gets my bill, he will have to give them up anyway!'

When you receive your miracle and the transformation of thought, be sure not to grab those old thoughts again. They never were you or yours, until you took ownership of them. They are only disempowering or negative energies, which are meant to just keep on flowing by.

Stuck Energy Can Move Again!

'The soul always knows what to do to heal itself. The challenge is to silence the mind.' —Caroline Myss

It is believed by many that it is stuck energy that causes lots of the health problems in our lives. Old traumas, negative beliefs, and unresolved issues, can remain stored in our beings and cells, causing blockages in the flow of our energy and thus pain, inflammation and other diseases.

Fortunately, there are healing modalities both old and many new, that have emerged and gained significant acceptance and success. Even modern medicine is starting to accept that these have a place in the range of solutions available. However, there is also a backlash from companies that would prefer their expensive pills and potions be considered as the only solutions.

In the west, we go to the doctor when we are sick; however, in ancient cultures especially the Chinese, the physician's job was to keep you healthy! From traditions and beliefs about our vital flows of energy, many healing methods have been found. Acupuncture, and the more modern EFT or tapping, are great examples along with Reiki, Quantum Touch, and many others.

Many modern miracles of healing have been accomplished just by a change of belief. There is an increase in awareness that pills for every eventuality, with so many of their side effects, are not the only or often even the best solution. In this world, we are starting to see and understand that all is composed of energy and vibrations, and run by thoughts, beliefs and expectations.

It is not the place in this book to delve too deeply into these ideas and methods, but it is important in maintaining your spacecraft to be aware that sometimes, the solution to malfunctioning parts can be found by addressing the deeper issues, righting core beliefs and unhealthy ideas. The very issues that have created the problems in the first place, can frequently be dissolved along with their manifested symptoms by many forms of energy healing.

I have come to the conclusion that, like so many other things on our journey here, much of what controls our smooth flights, is to do with our beliefs and attitudes. Correct them by whatever means possible and your spacecraft will be healed and well on its journey back to Love.

Stop Beating Yourself Up!

'Never regret. If it's good, it's wonderful. If it's bad, it's experience.' – Victoria Holt

If you do, you will wreck your spacecraft and quickly drain all the reserves of one the most important fuels of all, Happiness!

There is a verse in the Bible that says, 'Happy is the man that condemneth not himself for the thing which he alloweth', which could be translated as 'Stop beating yourself up!'

What is done is done! Remorse over the past is a completely futile exercise. It is done! This is especially true if we allow feelings of regret over any particular action that we love and hate in equal measures. Maybe we think this is bad for us, but then we love it so much, we just have to keep doing it? This could be smoking, overeating, or other excesses and addictions.

What to do? Change your thinking about the action! Either way, decide that the happiness generated by doing and enjoying it, is worth far more than any bad effect. Or, just decide it isn't worth doing because the effect is too bad. Get off the fence of indecision! This is a slippery slope with a crash, on either side! Make a decision! Then follow it, no matter what the old voices of habit and self-flagellation shout at you.

Okay, if it is potentially 'really' bad for you, maybe moderation could be exercised, or the better decision to cut it altogether. But if it doesn't hurt others, I am convinced that sometimes the happiness or pleasure generated has far more worth than many detriments. Now remember, this may not be true, but is sure a great belief and will lead to a far more enjoyable voyage for you and those around you.

Which is it for you: a long pained voyage of self-denial, or more pleasure and happiness that may appear to make for a shorter journey?

Failure or Another Disguised Step Forward

'Success is the ability to go from one failure to another without loss of enthusiasm.' – Winston Churchill.

I have another great belief that empowers me on this exciting journey. There is no such thing as failure! I will repeat it, as it's very important. *'There is no such thing as failure!'* Failure is just a bad way to view the seemingly unpleasant events of life! Are you in the middle of a perceived failure? If you can, take a step up, or into the secret place of your heart and then look down on the bigger picture.

The belief that we have planned everything before starting this voyage can be another powerful, happiness-holding belief, which, if truly believed, will give the perfect peace that *nothing* has gone wrong! After all, what spaceman on a very special voyage wouldn't have planned the route and all eventualities, as well as having lots of powerful backup systems in place? As already discussed, on this voyage we can choose our beliefs and truths. So grab this belief and keep it, ready for use, in your earth survival kit.

Yes, we can learn that there is a better way, but without that experience maybe we would have carried on down the same old and wrong road. So the lesson and knowledge gained becomes the growth factor, which proves the theory that there is no failure.

There have been plenty of roads in my life where all seemed like failure, dead ends loomed, and disasters played out their stories. At those times, it seemed like all was lost! However, in holding on, as life normally does, we pass through and life then brings its next changes. In the hindsight of looking back, life has always got better! —And if it doesn't seem like that for now, it is time to believe, look for, and step towards the next miracle.

Without these seeming disappointments or temporarily perceived failures, that next phase of growth, through change, could never have occurred! There is a wonderful promise you can claim. 'All things work together for good, to those who Love.'

There is no failing, only learning of other ways that didn't work, or that you chose not to pursue. It was once said that all roads lead to Rome and for us as Children of Spirit, all roads lead back to the Source! There are so many exciting experiences, lessons and growth opportunities along the way. So let's connect, touch other voyagers, play, have fun, and let Life itself flow through us.

'No' is Almost Never Personal

'You are good enough, smart enough, beautiful enough, strong enough. Believe it and stop letting insecurity run your life.' —Thema Davis

Were you ever laughed at or humiliated in school? The scars can run pretty deep, I know, especially after spending some time in private school, where humiliation seemed to be one of the favourite control mechanisms for many of the teachers. No wonder so many of us have struggled with close friendships or relationships and other areas of connecting with people. I think it is more of a male thing, as females generally have more of a natural bonding nature and ease of connection. I am sure though and have met many people of all genders who have had similar experiences and have carried those wounds and scars forward throughout their lives.

It's the subtle and underlying fears that have affected many of us, and become part of the beliefs and programmes that have now taken over. These fears can now run our subconscious decision-making programming, and thus take control of our actions.

The underlying fear of being made to look foolish or being humiliated, being shown to be wrong, or of failure—the list goes on and on. I am sure there is hardly a human who hasn't been affected to some degree by these fears. Now some compensate by hiding in self-erected shells or walls, distances designed to protect them; others overcompensate with pushy or obnoxious attitudes, creating the bully or Napoleon complex. Most of these reactions are a result of the same root cause.

It is time to realise how much these things can be holding us back; to learn that 'No' and rejection is never personal. It is so much more to do with the other person's programmes and beliefs, or the way they perceive us and our actions. Their actions, like our own, have been clouded by so many past experiences.

It's too easy to want to give up and hide behind the fortified walls we have built, which can become lonely ice-cold castles. In the worst case, they can leave us in a frozen Siberian winter. In our human journey, there is still that deep driving desire to connect, as underneath it all, we are gregarious creatures. We are on an even deeper level all one. Oh my, yet another human paradox, the need to connect and yet often being smothered by the fear of connection!

It is time to reprogramme that spacecraft. Change some of the beliefs, evict some of these out-of-control autopilots and fly back to Love.

Only Love can melt any lurking fears and insecurities. Is what's holding you back the fear of being told 'No', which most of us grew up with, as an almost staple diet? Let's journey back and show some kindness and love to that hurt inner child, understanding where we are coming from, in the realisation that we, too, have committed the same actions with others and whoever hurt us was also a victim of their own world experiences.

In most cases, attempting to do the right thing is a great start. Throw in some compassion and mix in even greater doses of Love for yourself and others. Soon the recipe is starting to smell and feel good, as it bakes in the warmth of your beautiful heart. Wow! Turn up the heat a bit more, burn away any old dross and maybe scrape off a few blackened bits, and the cake will be ready for icing, with lots of newfound sweetness in the great and coming feast of Love.

In our core, in energy, and essence, we are all Love! It just remains for us to pass through all the processes and experiences of this journey, to purify and cleanse us again. We will all, in time, return to that pure state of being, leaving behind all past sad experiences and fears like old clothes, dirty and torn. They are not us, just experiences and facilitators of choice and decision. They help us to see, understand and choose what we really want, what our inner heart and being cries out for. Isn't it great to know that there is nothing that can enter the heart of man, no thought or desire, which this powerful universe cannot deliver? This is especially true for any desire for cleansing, freedom, and growth. Let us return again to the powerful truth that *'Life Loves Us.'* I am convinced that when we have all got tired of the many games and illusions of this journey, we are all destined to return to that place and Being of unlimited Love.

What Are You Looking For and What Do You Notice?

'Was it a bad day? Or was it a bad five minutes that you milked all day?' – Author unknown

It's a beautiful day; the sun is shining, and you are happily driving your vehicle past a stunning park full of beautiful flowers and suddenly, someone cuts in in front of you! The alarm bells in your head go off! What a bleep! Anxiety levels rise, indignation pours out and something just short of road rage follows. You might even stew about it for a while, and even complain to your companion about the others lousy driving. Or maybe it's a shop with poor customer service that ruffled your feathers, so much that a letter of complaint is envisioned, if not actioned, as this terrible injustice fills your thoughts and consciousness for hours.

You are probably right and that natural reaction is a part of our old programming. In the early days of man, if we didn't watch out for trouble and when seen, act on it and then run, we could end up becoming some bigger creatures next dinner. The trouble is that now, maintaining such a high state of anxiety over a long period is extremely bad for us, in this very different age! Somehow, through just one incident, we will have long forgotten the beautiful day and enjoying the journey, or the great service we received in all the other shops.

Pause, take some deep breaths and decide: is this experience what you really want to focus on? Then make your choice and fly your craft back into the sunshine. Our journey here is too short to mar it with the weights, which the person who may have committed such an atrocity, will never feel anyway!

Improve It! Don't Attempt to Fix It!

'Give yourself a gift of five minutes of contemplation in awe of everything you see around you. Go outside and turn your attention to the many miracles around you. This five-minute-a-day regimen of appreciation and gratitude will help you to focus your life in awe.' —Wayne Dyer

We have all been programmed to look for what is wrong, and then figure out how we can fix it. Remember though, what we focus on expands, so if not checked, our whole experience could soon be full of things needing fixing!

I spent eighteen months working with a great mentor, John Milton Fogg. One of the most important lessons from that time was driven into habit by the daily activities of a call with an accountability buddy. There were a series of questions designed to change our focus from what's wrong to what's working. What did we like? What would we like? What could be even better and how could we improve our experiences? This is powerful life-changing work, which resulted in attaining many desires and goals. More important than that, it also changed and reprogrammed the habitual focus of looking for all the wrongs to fix.

How many times does that voice in our head rattle on about all the things that are wrong with us, and our circumstances? Or maybe we have reached a higher level of self-righteousness and the voice mainly complains about the actions and attitudes of those around us? Or worse yet, about all the grief and troubles in our lives and their causes then firmly planted on others, and so many things and circumstances.

It's time to make changes! What is working for you?

Exercise: Make a list of what is working for you, dwell on it for a while, and then cement its effect with a generous coating of gratitude. Repeat the process a few times a day for several days and then take stock of how your mood and feelings have lifted.

Working Your Way to Heaven Won't Work!

- Let's get back to simply Loving!

'In the end, only three things matter: How much you loved, how gently you lived, and how gracefully you let go of things not meant for you.' – Buddha

Whether it is a strict meditation routine, never missing mass or any other ritual or repetitive practice, those should or should not's; these are all just other religions—your attempts to become perfect, to answer an inner guilt.

Loving along the route of a fun-filled, joyous life journey, shedding that guilt with forgiveness, laughter and love, this is the path of enlightenment! Making the journey lighter, until all burdens, shoulds, musts, and feelings of unworthiness, just drop off and float away. You are a child of Love and Life. Your birthright is the key to a life of Love forever, not some works trip, seeking an elusive state of perfection—that if truth were known and remembered—you already have! After all, who can make perfect a dream?

Why do we strive so, when Life and Love are a gift, waiting to unfold; as we awake, remember, and open to accept them? The secret is to Love—yourself especially, and all those that bring the lessons, as our reflections. And sometimes, for the stronger seemingly more horrible ones, the lessons can be passed and learnt through a more powerful incantation of Love; 'I'm sorry, please forgive me, thank you, I love you!' These words are the core of an ancient Hawaiian healing practice, called Ho'oponopono.

Yes, some practices, rituals and forms of worship can be steps on the route to realisation, but too often they become just another work's trip, the musts on a downward circle of self-righteousness, an impossible seeking of human perfection. That is the impossible dream, which is often sold by those seeking to control us, or accumulate our wealth! These are often old or new religions, selling the works for salvation, seemingly quick fixes at a price!

Love is the solution, becoming childlike again in the simplicity of Love; the uplifting of Joy with childlike faith and gratitude; that is Life itself, which has bestowed the greatest gift of the being, of a priceless part of Divinity, on each part of itself, which is Us.

Shit Happens!

'People change, things go wrong, shit happens, but life goes on!' —Shamila Ali

Eating can be a pleasurable, wonderful experience: An exceptionally delicious tasty meal with a glass of your favourite drink, beautiful music transporting you into deep connection with a close friend or lover. One can hardly imagine a more pleasant experience. Later, our space ship processes it, and extracts the goodness and nutrients. It stores the wonderfully nourishing memories and then throws away the waste. Shit comes out! We accept this as normal and move on.

Yet when we go through life and are presented with learning experiences, with the potential to extract lessons, and potentially growing in understanding, the shit comes out. Why do we sometimes choose to wallow in it for days and often, at that time, decide these are bad experiences? How much better could we feel, if we chose to believe and programme ourselves that these were empowering growth experiences, letting the shit come out and move on, rather than choosing to stay stuck, wallowing in the pity party and the consequences of the decision or meaning we made, that this was a bad experience?

Hold On! The Crown, the Fruit, and the Rewards Are On Their Way!

'Never, Never, Never, Never give up.' —Winston Churchill

There are so many examples of persistence, dogged determination, and faith, eventually bringing forth desired results, even after seeming defeats that it's difficult to know which to recount. It's amazing how often, after that seeming defeat, followed by that tenacious human tendency to stick it out, there comes great victory. It seems that a part of our growing process is the testing of our resolve. That testing often comes before the universe can reward us with our ultimate desires and blessings.

Frequently, the largest goals or the highest mountains bring on the toughest tests! Like Jim Rohn shared, the man who says, 'I will climb that mountain, I will not return, unless I reach that peak. I will attain my goal, or die in the process,' he is the one, which the universe decides to allow to reach that pinnacle of success.

A story in my garden comes to mind, as a recent colourful example. I love strawberries. Do you? Their succulent taste, the delicious smell, the bright red colour of this exquisite fruit heralds the start of our summer. They bring joyous recollection of childhood pleasures and memories of exciting strawberry picking adventures. Anyway, enough meandering down the path picking daisies, or was it strawberries?

I had bought some lovely, promising strawberry plants last year. They were growing in pots on my sunny windowsill, starting to flower, and full of the promise of their soon coming, juicy fruits. Then disaster struck; almost overnight, their bright healthy green leaves turned a horrid dry brown. Their life forces were fading away. Even taking them outside didn't help. All but three of the nine plants were soon completely stone dead. The last three were left desperately struggling to cling to life and their inbuilt purpose, to produce fruit. Just three tiny undernourished and poor little strawberries emerged. Then in time, a few runners slowly came forth, as these tenacious little plants kept on, with the growth of their purpose to reproduce and bring forth fruit. I tended these precious growths, giving them little posts of fresh soil. By the start of this year, there were now twelve little plants. They were then lovingly planted out, into a sunny corner of my garden.

In the warm sunlight—of the loving rays of our majestic sun—there little plants, once barely hanging onto life, have now majestically grown and thrived. They have brought forth an abundance of their wonderful fruits, my and their rewards, for holding on and not giving up that life force, the dream, and inbuilt programming to succeed and prosper.

Another touching story comes to mind. It is more of a warning though, but still shows how that crown is always there, just waiting for our resolve to reach it.

In the days of brutal communist persecution, three Christians were to face the ultimate test in the depth of Siberia's bitterest winter after already enduring the harshest hells of a vicious labour camp. These three faced a final trial of their faith. They were dragged onto an ice flow, stripped naked and told: 'Now renounce your faith or die. Or embrace communism, then you can live and be free to return to society.' They had just moments to live and make that toughest of decisions.

As he watched his companions pass the threshold into death, the last one wavered and croaked, 'I do.' Then the strangest thing happened, a young guard throws off his clothes and cries, 'Take my rifle and overcoat. Just as you faltered, I saw two mighty angels about to put a crown on your head. I will take your place, I want that crown!' One man loses his crown, and another receives it!

I wonder how many great inventions, how many victories in the heat of battle, how many personal success stories, would not exist; and where our civilisation would be, if it were not for that tenacious persistence that can live in the heart of our beings?

I truly believe there is no desire that can enter our consciousness and our wonderful hearts that this universe of thinking matter cannot manifest into our earthly voyage.

The results and the coronation is not our job. Our work is the preparation, the resolve, the 'being there till the bell rings', and then the rewards will follow in their own perfect time.

Can you see it? Have you heard it? Do you feel it? The next time you are tested, look deep within; call out for the resolve, and hold on for that wonderful victory—it is there waiting to bless your faith. The inbuilt power of the life within can carry you through to every victory and the ultimate fulfilment of your desires, purpose, and destiny.

It's time for the 'What If Game' – Review Questions

Here are some questions derived from the last section to give the chance to review and enhance your learnings. Play it, if you like, by taking some time out to ponder on the answers that will come when you get quiet.

Some of the questions are now also becoming 'What could be the result if you . . .' This is another powerful way of exploring possibilities.

What if there was more time to listen to the still small voice in my heart, rather than the louder voices that sometimes make the most noise?

What if there was time to take a deep breath, before accepting the first meaning that comes to my mind, when things next appear to go wrong?

What if I determined to write down all the quotes that powerfully spoke to me and reviewed them a couple of times a day for the next thirty days, or longer if it appears to be empowering?

What if I became the observer, looking at my thoughts and letting those that don't serve just pass through, rather than inviting them in for tea?

What if it was easily possible to let go of things that may trouble me?

What if I made the decision to make a gratitude list?

What if healing was possible and a change of attitude could speed its progress?

What if I banished regret and learnt to trust in the wonder of now?

What if the ray of light and purpose in each failure became apparent?

What if I decided to never take rejection personally?

What if I found a way to shed like the water off a duck's back, all thoughts that would otherwise bring me down?

What if it was easy to spend more time looking to improve life, rather than looking for problems to fix?

What if there were no rituals, only acceptance of the gift of Life's Love?

What if more ways came to me to find gratitude in every situation?

What if I discovered what could happen by finding the grace to hold on that bit longer in trying times?

SECTION 3

Taking Control

Take Responsibility!

'It's always easy to blame others. You can spend your entire life blaming the world, but your successes and failures are entirely your own responsibility.' – Paulo Coelho

When we live in a word of blame and this becomes our reality, then of course, we are powerless to change or affect things, as everything that happens is believed to be beyond our control! By this time, we have succumbed to the inevitable despondency that the world is a terrible place and everything is conspiring to get us; there is no hope, etc. and on and on it goes, in a downward spiral to a self (or was it others) made hell.

How about if we reprogrammed that spacecraft with the diametrically opposite belief? That we are in some way responsible for everything that happens in our lives? That is, every result, each situation, and especially our attitudes and the meanings we take from each experience. Could this help our flight levels of success, happiness, and the direction we are flying in?

It's not necessarily true, but for a moment, let's consider a more empowering belief: that you are the cause of everything, or to believe that you are under the control of the effects of everything around you. Which craft is more likely to succeed? The one flying through a loving universe that is helping look after the flight plan and destination, giving the ultimate choices to its pilot; or the craft that is flying through a dark world, where everything conspires against it, no intervention and guidance from the centre, and no control of direction? That is a flight plan where an almost certain, ultimate fate is to crash and burn!

Most successful and happy people I know have adopted a similar belief. It's amazing how—even if isn't completely true—such a belief empowers and gives a measure of control, even over many of our journey's most difficult challenges.

Ask How

'The important thing is not to stop questioning.' – Albert Einstein

This writing bug is something else! Dring . . . Dring . . . Dring . . . It's 3.30 in the morning, anyone else would think it's just the phone going flat but it was . . . Mission Control calling—get up and write!

They say that nature abhors a vacuum. At least that's what I seem to remember my physics master banging on about, way back in school.

I'm actually now convinced that nature and spirit love a vacuum. Yes—they love to fill it! Any time there is a sincere desire or question, the answer will come—maybe not always in the form or time scale that we were expecting, but the answer is always there.

Do you need the answer to some deep question? Use the Law of Attraction. Get quiet and from the centre of your deep desire and beautiful heart, sincerely ask the magic question: How? Then listen and watch in quietness and confidence—without presupposition, without impatience—and the answer will almost always be there or be arriving soon, sometimes in the most magical of ways.

Often too, this same principle—mixed with faith, intention, and expectation—can work to attract the things we desire into our lives. Though sometimes, because of the period of gestation of the seed of your desire, it may take longer to grow and manifest in full than your faith can stand. Then, when doubt slips in its fears and contrary beliefs, they may hinder the process.

Mission Control for the space fleet is in most cases in great radio communication, and looking to answer our questions or send a supply craft with our needs. It's just that sometimes we are a little further away from the centre and it can take a bit longer, or there is a temporary electric storm of those fears and disbelief disrupting communications; or maybe, just for a while, we are passing on the dark side of the moon.

What Does It Take to Become Free?

'You begin to fly when you let go of self-limiting beliefs and allow your mind and aspirations to rise to greater heights.' — Brian Tracy

Many voyages are blighted by so many limiting beliefs, and the collection of voices that cry out deep in our subconscious.

It takes breaking the ties that bind and the walls that have been built up by habitually following these voices. The beliefs from these voices have been imposed over our lifetimes and even before, from our ancestors.

What can we do? First, realise that not all the voices and beliefs are yours, or empowering your voyage, or letting you travel where you may want to go. I'd suggest a deep soul searching, and then taking time to write down the thoughts from the voices you hear and the beliefs that are at the forefront or even in the depths of your being.

The great thing about beliefs is they are not true! They are just accumulated thoughts, repeated time and time again until they become the strong chords and habits that frequently restrict our actions and beings.

What would you like to believe? Believe it or not, you can choose! Wouldn't it be so much more powerful to craft a series of your own beliefs, which can help you fly in the directions of your choice and experience the fullness of your desires? Yes safety is important—but remember that the divine creature flying your earthly craft is indestructible and immortal.

Take a go at writing down the opposite of any of the limiting beliefs you discover and drilling and experimenting with these. If they work, then adopt them, if not, throw them out. It doesn't hurt to experiment and experience. Over time you can challenge and overcome any of the limits as to how you can fly your craft!

Two Things That Will Crash Your Spacecraft

'When you judge another, you don't define them, you define yourself!' – Wayne Dyer

Judgement is a terrible thing! In comparing ourselves with others, we are either lifting ourselves up in self-righteousness and puffing up our ego—which doesn't need it—or we are demeaning ourselves and therefore sealing our place in a morass of low self-esteem and failing self-confidence.

So many of the world's ills have come about because people have been sold the idea that they are better than others and thus more worthy of resources, forgiveness, land, or life. Whether religion, political leaders, or just the voice in your head, it's time to put aside judgement and take a big dose of respect, both for yourself—as the amazing being you are—and for the other and their value as another part of our human family.

Another form of judgement could be held in the beliefs passed down through generations, which we have swallowed and regurgitated as our own—maybe just as almost subconscious thoughts that still control our feelings. 'Rich people are evil.' 'To have that wealth they must be crooks.' 'Look at that poverty—they must be lazy.' 'What did they do to get that?' 'How could they do that?' Unless we can walk a mile with each person, we will never know the depth of their thoughts, sufferings, or what makes them tick, let alone their motivation or what events have affected their lives. Each time we point a finger, let's remember the other four are pointing right back at us!

We will find that life flows so much more smoothly when we look at each other as equals, looking for the best in people and situations—not how we are better or worse than them— but realising we have much to learn from everyone that crosses our path.

'As I walked out the door towards the gate that would lead to my freedom, I knew if I didn't leave my bitterness and hatred behind, I'd still be in prison.' – Nelson Mandela

Beware of *bitterness*! There is not much worse for the peace and harmony of our journey than embracing or holding on to bitterness. Revenge or the old beliefs of 'an eye for an eye' have set off wars that have destroyed generations.

Again, the solution is about taking responsibility on our journey, and realising that we have allowed, created, or been at cause for all of the events that befall us. This choice can be hard to comprehend and believe, but I'm sure it's the best attitude and belief to hold, to ensure a smooth flight through life.

If you can't step out this far in your beliefs, at the very least, be sure not to hold the grudges and festering sores of bitterness. This attitude won't hurt the person you're blaming or deem responsible, but it will rob you of all joy, love, and peace—and continue over time to sap your very health and essence.

There comes a point in life where if we are to grow, we must take control of and abandon many of the old ways, and base emotions that we were taught, or had adopted as a part of mankind's early fight for survival. There is no way to 'Fly Back to Love' if we are still carrying the burdens and weights of the past.

Forgiveness, even if a tough pill, is the key to healing and to a life once again flowing in harmony. If needed, take that step and you will soon see how your spirit and emotions will lift— just from shedding the weights that have previously held you back.

Two Enemies of a Smooth Ride, in the Right

'If you are depressed, you are living in the past. I anxious, you are living in the future. If you are at peace, you are living in the present.' – Lao Tzu

Let's take a look at the two biggest destroyers and enemies of peace, joy and happiness. They are remorse over the past and fear about the future. Let's zoom in on each one right now.

The Past.

First is the bad news that there is nothing we can do to actually change our past, as it has already happened and has already been written. Now, here is the good news. There is a lot we can do to change our perception of the events of the past. These recollections are probably so distorted already in our memories and what we consider as 'the facts' about what happened. The events are already lost in the shifting sands of time, and everyone who experienced them actually has a different picture, experience, and perception. So what makes us so determined to be right about our own particular version?

Why would we choose remorse or regret, or the even potentially more damaging desires for revenge or retribution? These repeated thoughts, which are energy, then create emotions or energies in motion. The trouble is, in most cases, that that kind of energy becomes stuck in these lower vibrations and then it can spiral downward in a blocked loop, creating in its wake disease and stealing all our joy and gratitude. Or in the worse cases, it can lead to even more regretted actions. These lower vibrations are stealing and blinding us to all the wonders and potentials of the glorious now!

What to do is shockingly simple! *Let go!* Look for ways to change your focus, guard against, and root out from what could be the beautiful garden of your mind any seeds of those repeating thoughts that seek to keep you looking backwards instead of looking at today in wonder and gratitude.

Watch out for rose coloured glasses, distorting old memories, or increasing perceptions that the grass is greener elsewhere. Remember, it still must be mowed!

The past is gone! Whatever it was, even if you could still see it clearly, it is already written. We could choose to waste time and energy tied up in our perception of the losses, remaining stuck, considering what we missed, or how we did it wrong; or if we did it better, what could have happened. But what could this possibly benefit? It is over!

Let's make the decision to just face it one last time, and acknowledge it's gone. If needed, let's send the healing kisses of 'I'm sorry, please forgive me. Thank you, I love you', to our past self or others we may have hurt. Then it is time to turn again and embrace the present '*now*', knowing that this is where we are now and live; and the only place we can work the miracles of creation and change.

So let's move on and consider **The Future**.

Again, too many people spend the hours of their days stuck in thinking—or almost meditating—about their self-limiting perceptions of a troubled future, or even perceived lacks, and other insecurities that they imagine are soon to befall them. Self-limiting fears and visualised troubles can soon become self-fulfilling prophesies of what surely might happen if . . .

Stop here and fill in the blanks. Then pause and take a look: is this what you really want? If it is, great! If it isn't, please stop! Yes, stop thinking about it as, *'thoughts create things!'* The chances are—if you keep thinking about these things, they could very well become a part of your next reality.

Focus now and take the time to think about what you really would like. It is much more productive and has the power to take you on your voyage to far better places.

If you don't know, ask Spirit and Life in their greater wisdom to take you to the places of their highest good. Then stop worrying and trust the process. This is the purpose and intent of Life anyway, and I believe would just unfold naturally if we'd just get out of the way and stop messing it up with so many regrets, fears, and low or stuck vibrations.

Yes it's time now in our evolution to let go. Let's stop our efforts through our limited human perceptions and the ego that demands to be in control. Let's flow into the master plan that is waiting to unfold and thrill us, in the wonder of its beauty. I believe, we, at a higher level were there, involved in the planning of our life anyway. It's just that we have chosen to temporarily forget those plans, but that is another story or message for another time!

So what about the *now*? Yes, right now! What if we could just be here? Which we are, anyway! So let's focus on this moment, with presence and gratitude, with our eyes wide open to its wonders, its beauty, its promise and its potential. It is the birthing place of all things and the crucible of creation, which can—if we just let it—lift our vibrations into higher spheres of experience and abiding joys. Wow! Let's go together on that voyage, stepping into the brighter and lighter future in the right now.

What do You Fill and Programme Your World With?

'We become what we think about most of the time, and that's the strangest secret.' – Earl Nightingale

Imagine for a moment how you would feel and react if your best friend arrived, carrying a big sack. He then came straight into your living room, or worse yet, your bedroom and proceeded to scatter the contents of his sack—blood, guts, gore and nasty creatures—all around. He then goes on to paint on your walls scenes of disaster, famine and pestilence, before saying a curt goodnight and leaving.

Would you tolerate that for a second, especially if your children were in the room? Would you have called the police? Would you ever have spoken to him again? A banning order may be appropriate!

Yet so many of us start the day with the news, on the radio or TV, and then finish it with another big dose before bed. I know previously, some years ago, I did. In my hunger to keep up with all that was going on. I would spend, probably an hour or two, or more addicted to the latest information, with my fix first thing in the morning, a boost at lunchtime, and a final shot just before sleeping. No wonder my world was full of conflict and fears. It was what I was inviting in!

Now maybe it's not that bad for you, though I'm sure, the mind-numbing drivel and titillating experiences through many soaps—or the superficial chatter on much of social media—isn't doing much to inspire and nourish the lives of the masses. That box, whether a tablet, computer, or the TV in the corner of so many rooms, can seriously steal and control our lives.

Now that doesn't mean that all entertainment is bad. A break, an escape to relax, a journey of emotions, different experiences, through a good film or series can be fun and another way to recharge especially where the story and principle characters have values and play out great lessons in their dramas.

I have heard it asked, 'Why would you want to spend so much of your time, watching other people getting wealthy, playing out their or your dreams, when you could be playing out your own dreams in the blockbuster of your life?'

Of course, there is a balance, and some relaxation is great. The big questions should be, are you taking the time to feed your mind with positive material, thoughts, and the programming that will help you grow, and take you to where you want to travel? Are you taking time to still your mind and reach the quiet places of your heart and soul with meditation? Are you taking time to connect deeply with those around you, and also to nourish your body with healthy exercise?

Wise men say, we are, or become the average of the people we associate with, in wealth, and quality of life, and thought. If you can't actually be with some of the really great people that you would like to meet, how about reading their books, or listening to their audio programmes, or webinars, and taking time to experience their workshops?

I once had the life-changing experience of a 30-day mental fast. No news, or newspapers, no TV or radio, just edifying books, audio programmes or personal development materials. It was quite profound—how like the false appetite for junk food wears off after an extended cleansing detox, my desire and addiction for much of those materials also vanished. Part of the magic is the thirty days, as it takes that long to purge old habits and refresh them with new ones. The start of a holiday and its total break with routine is a great way to start this process, if you are thinking of experiencing it.

We are what we eat, and we become like all we associate with! Let's be fully aware and choose wisely, all the things and actions that create our worlds.

Be Careful What You Focus On!

'The key to success is to focus our conscious mind on the things we desire not things we fear.' – Brian Tracy

Do you think about what you really want? Or do those stray thoughts, which float by, start to build new realities of their own in your world—before you are fully aware of what they are creating?

Be aware, thoughts become and create things! We are creation machines and we often don't realise the powers we are wielding—they shape the world we live in! Our thoughts, mixed with the energy of emotions, become our intentions, which, in turn become our manifestations.

Is it a little fear, or ill-conceived thought that at first seems almost harmless? Yet it can soon start to take root. Or is it a desire that slowly becomes an all-encompassing purpose. Be aware—many of these things can be either good or bad depending on what we really want, and their outcomes. The powerful force of driving thoughts has created empires, and has been the source of many human achievements. They have also created addictions, misused power or jealousies and off-centred or unbalanced worlds, taking their original perpetrators far from the places of their first intentions.

Are you in control of your thoughts, or are they running you? Are they usually taking you places and creating the experiences you deeply desire, or do they often seem to have a mind of their own and lead to embarrassment, anger or loss? Just as it is important to set a watch before our lips and create uplifting words, it is vitally important to be aware of the thoughts, which first create those words and actions. It is said that the power of life and death is in the tongue and the words it sends forth. However before every word is thought, those thoughts are having their way, in creating our reality, long before any words are uttered!

Now, maybe one little thought isn't going to accomplish much, but as soon as it gets repeated, then it has a friend, and as the power of two sets in, they begin to work together and invite a few more to join them. Is it critical? Is it jealous? Is it fearful? Or is it greedy? Soon, they build their patterns and a neural web is forming, a habit is growing, a powerful net of thought, repeating and repeating, chains that bind and build actions— these are often far different than the original intentions of your pure heart.

Is there any hope? Yes, the good news is, the same process works with all thoughts; purposely constructed thoughts will lift you to places where you'd like to go. This kind—you can be fully in control of! Take time to become aware of where your thoughts and actions could be leading! Consider what they are creating and then exercise your greatest human power, the majesty of choice.

Is that thought creating a slippery road you don't want to go down? Is that where you want to live and a route you'd like to follow? Can you see where this thought pattern might be taking you, or has already brought you? Are the results growing and sometimes causing frequent discomfort? Are alarm bells ringing? Is disease taking its hold? Is your world changing from the place of joy—our birth right—to a dull, grey, sad place, far from where it you'd like to belong and live?

Now all changes come from decisions and sometimes it can be just as simple as that. The miracle is the change of heart or direction. In other cases where everything seems completely overpowering, is it time to ask *Love* for the power and help to change things? See the next topic 'Sincere Heart Cry Can Change Your World.'

Either way: step in with new thoughts of gratitude, thoughts of desires, of what you really like to create. Yes, change is possible, but it will take some work, re-patterning those old thought patterns and neural nets. Use the repetition of affirmations and new desires. Spend time, carefully tending the garden of your mind, ripping out old weeds and planting the beautiful flowers of desired creations. Beautiful flowers and perfect creations all start with very small seeds of thought. They need tending and watering, feeding, and protecting from any old weeds, which may be looking to spring up and choke them. Make sure you know the difference, and watch carefully for those weeds. Root them out, at the first sign that they may be pretenders, creeping into the garden of your mind. Feed and repeat many life-giving affirmations and every positive thought you can plant. The more you plant, the less chance of space for any weeds to enter in.

I am healthy. I am happy. I am Love. I create my genuine desires. I create a beautiful world based on real values, with powerful thoughts of good and great intentions. Pleasure and love grow for me and everything and everyone in my world.

Repeat these affirmations frequently and many others like them. These new thoughts will then grow and become the things that create and fill your world. New thoughts will create new thought patterns, and unexpected new roads to the places of your desires. Just give them a chance, and the time it takes for them to grow and build.

Sincere Heart Cry, Can Change Your World

'When the world pushes you to your knees, yo
perfect position to pray.' – Rumi

Have you ever been in that place where everything seems to be closing in? That dream, that goal, your heartfelt desire, seems to be slipping away into oblivion? Darkness surrounds, and the end of what you had dreamed, or even believed was seemingly nigh? Once what was progress and hope, now slipping backwards into defeat—happiness fleeing and your previously bright world is now a fading hope, just a distant glimmer of that once bright joyful light.

Don't give up! Never quit! It is time to find a quiet spot within, or without, whether a mountaintop or a bed in the night, or a quiet closet. It is a strange thing, but yes, even for men, it's okay to cry. In fact, pause for a moment and think: when was the last time you cried? If it's tough and you need it, here is your permission. Its washing is cathartic!

It's time to bare your heart, cry out for your dreams, and show your resolve, clinging onto your beliefs and desires. It's time to wrestle, with the proverbial angel deep inside, in heartfelt tears of sincerity and desire. Let your cry and prayer resonate throughout your being, and echo into the deepest places of your universe. From this place, I know it is always heard and has the power to change anything and everything in your world!

Now there is one small caveat: one thing we must be aware of and also be open too. As our human understanding is not yet perfect, the answer may not always be exactly what we expect. Though from experience in most cases, I have found it is—as the deepest desires of my heart have usually been aligned with my purpose and direction. Whatever it is, and is best for us, will, surely come!

Little prayers are all well and good, but there is nothing like a deep cleansing heart cry to change the situation. There are times to surrender, crying Abba Father to that deepest part of your being—the loving part, which is in control of all. That prayer from the deepest part of your beautiful, sincere heart and being will always result in victory! Then it is time to dry your tears, and know the answer—however it is packaged, is on its way. You can then watch for and experience the miracle.

I have been in similar places numerous times in my life, some were deeper and more desperate situations; some seeming smaller, yet still over important things. I know, without fail, those turning points have come through that place of heart cry—most of them with tears, and the complete nakedness of heartfelt expression and surrender.

Sometimes, there has been a beautiful sign even before the answer arrived that I had been heard, and the answer was on its way. Once I was on a beautiful country hill crying out, over a particularly trying situation. When I reached that magic point of knowing that it was done, wiping the tears from my eyes, I saw in the grass just next to me; what appeared to be a snake—suddenly fear raised its ugly head within. However, I soon saw, it was just an empty snakeskin—just like the lies and fears that had surrounded me. All that was really there were empty fears! And life from that point changed, bringing back once again my desires and hopes. They then appeared to be within my reach once more, and I was back on my path again in faith.

Another time as that heart cry ended, I picked up a holy book and from the very first pages that opened, in a few paragraphs, was the story of my quest. Then the answers unfolded with the message: 'Wait on the Lord, be of good courage and he shall strengthen thy heart.' Sometimes, there is a loud answer; and at other times, just the quiet, still, small voice of confidence within that breaks through the storm, with the knowing that all is well.

A recent example of this beautiful cleansing, and life-changing heart cry process, is shared in my story and blog entry called 'Loves' Collisions.'

It is all about the change of our perception or beliefs. The miracle is that magic moment when the darkness flees; when we turn back to the light, and once again can focus on all that is Love and light. Then the miracle is free to manifest. It sometimes takes that stripping back, that heart cry, the washing in the tears of desire, the realignment with our inner being, and declaration of our purpose, to once again move us forward. *'Life Loves You'* and is waiting to manifest its perfection!

Whatever the trial, whatever the dark situation is for you, know that deep within—in that secret place—there is always an answer waiting for you. Your tears of surrender and heart cry, if needed, can always find it!

Change Is Just One Heartbeat Away . . . But?

'It takes deep commitment to change, and an even deeper commitment to grow.' – Ralph Ellison

Which would you like first: the good news or the bad news? The good news: change happens in a heartbeat. The bad news: it usually takes commitment, effort, and determination to make it stick.

The big questions are: do you believe it, and do you really want it?

Failure to believe, or especially believing the opposite that you can't do it, or that it won't work, will hinder or completely halt the process. That is, until the underlying beliefs and autopilot programmes are changed.

Either way, you believe something; and either way, it's not true until you make it so! That is the catch twenty-two of the two parts of the equation! Beliefs always come before and control action!

The great news is that when you are ready, and your heart cries out in true sincerity—the answer is on the way. That, from personal experience, often involves a breaking in desperation, being washed by a flood of tears, and a total soul-felt desire and commitment to change. Then that desire from your core being, and the magnetic inbuilt pull of your purpose and destiny will unleash unbeatable forces to guide you through the changes and onward on your journey.

It's not rocket science! When your desire to change is mixed with belief and some skills and actions, it then becomes greater than the inertia of the old habits, programmes, and beliefs. Then that marvellous change can happen in a heartbeat!

There is more in the section 'Letting Go', but for now let's put the question: *'Do you really want it?'* under a magnifying glass.

Often, there can be a small desire to change; but frequently, it's not big enough to tip the balance of inertia and the benefits of staying the same. There is a price to pay—giving up the old and somewhat comfortable ways for an unknown new. Or maybe the sympathy and attention of the old seems more worthwhile than the effort, challenges, and uncertainties of change and a new life.

This could be similar to people stuck on minimal government benefits and they would have to give them up to start some new, risky business or job. It's like an old but familiar, unsatisfying—or worse yet—abusive relationship. Or maybe a sickness that brings the benefit of extra care and attention. It can be difficult and scary to make the changes needed for a healing or for the new life that is dreamed of, but still seems almost a step too far.

Yes, some way or another we have to die to make changes happen. It takes dying to the old, and stepping into a new uncertain future. The old has to become almost unbearable before most of us are willing to take that step of faith. Sometimes though, this lack of decision and action results in some seemingly disastrous circumstances. These can push us over the edge of the precipice into the now inevitable change. At the time it can seem like a disaster—even the end of a world—but looking back later, can often be viewed as a blessing in disguise.

Life has its own way of guiding us into what is good for us! Sometimes when we don't listen and follow those little checks, it can send bigger and more powerful messages, or an eventual earthquake to completely shake us out of the old ruts, and stuck or negative situations. The storm is tough at the time, but wait, and there is always a rainbow or silver lining to that once dark cloud.

There is a great story that many have told, but maybe you haven't yet heard it, or if you have it could be good to consider again. An old dog sits, constantly whimpering and moaning on the porch. A well-meaning animal lover seeks to help. After several days when passing by seeing this suffering dog, he calls in to ask its owner what the problem is, and could he help in some way. He was surprised by the answer. The dog is sitting on a nail. Dumbfounded, he asks, 'Why?' And the answer: 'The discomfort just doesn't hurt him enough to move yet!'

Let's hope that your desire will well up enough, and the benefits will outweigh all the inertia to make that decision in a heartbeat, and then stick with it long enough to take the needed steps to make it happen. You will then find and live the new life you desire and reap the joys of watching it unfold.

In olden times, a wise general, taking his army to a new land, had crossed the sea in boats. After his men had landed and set up their new camp, he ordered the boats burnt, so that there was no way to go back. That way, he knew, they would give their all to survive and press forward. With no chance of fleeing to a comfortable past—they had to win the battle! This is sometimes what it takes! Before new futures can be founded, absolute commitment is required! Beware, it's often too easy to look back and then the old can suddenly take on a strangely different and rosy glow!

So yes, change happens in a heartbeat; and desire with absolute commitment; and no looking back can cement it into your new reality.

There Is an Ancient Practice That Can Change Your World

'If you want to change what's going on around you, change what's going on within you.' – Billy Cox

This practice is a powerful mixture of mindfulness, taking responsibility, forgiveness, gratitude, and love.

It has empowered, touched my journey, and proved a special tool to answer and to help melt back into the void many situations, experiences, and some of the horrors that lurk in the dark corners of this world.

In this form it originated in Hawaii, though I am sure many other life-changing tools incorporate the same principles. I will only cover it briefly, and I would recommend investigating it more thoroughly if it resonates with you. One route is through Joe Vitale's excellent books *'Zero Limits'* and *'At Zero.'*

This practice was brought into our present world by a medical practitioner, Dr Ihaleakala Hew Len. He emptied a worst offender prison in Hawaii using the power of its practice. It is called Ho'oponopono.

The simple and powerful mantra or prayer 'I'm sorry. Please forgive me. Thank you. I love you,' can change your world! I use it when anything so absolutely horrible—that it is almost unbelievable—enters my world. These are the kinds of atrocities that would have put these insane felons into that hospital for the criminally insane in the first place. They are the kind of acts that the newspapers seem to love to spread— often titillating our human attraction for disasters and the morbid. In the process, they are spreading many fears into our world and consciousness.

There is tremendous power in taking responsibility and acknowledging that I—as a human being—am capable of, and have possibly committed similar atrocities in thought or dream, action, or maybe even in other lifetimes. The extremes of darkness and light are in each of us!

Another process that uses similar principles is Dr John Demartini's *'Forgiveness Process.'* This process is again an experience of cleansing. By taking responsibility, the process can make momentous changes in the meaning placed and carried by traumatic experiences. Like Ho'oponopono, it is also based on the acknowledgement of our own responsibility and humanity.

'I'm sorry. Please forgive me. Thank you. I love you.' They are so simple, powerful, cleansing and transforming words. The power of life and death is in the power of the tongue. The healing words that the tongue can speak will melt any atrocity and wash away its power, and the fears that power is wrapped in, cleansing, and making whole again. Can you believe it? Investigate it for yourself. Check out the power of that heart cry and prayer—especially when resonating from the core of your beautiful, mindful being.

Take a look at your thoughts from the centre of your being. Realise they are not you or yours, but thoughts that have swirled around this universe for years. Shine the light of your truth on them. Are they real or imaginary? Remember, there only exists Love or fear. Be the observer. Let go and fly by those thoughts that don't serve the Love you are. Remember, *'Life Loves You'* and your core is Love. Fear not! Nothing can harm you!

No More Trying—Just Do It!

'Try not. Do . . . or do not. There is no try!' – Yoda

Would you be happy and full of confidence if the pilot of your plane suddenly announced, "We have a small problem here, but don't worry, we are going to try to land the plane?"

Or if you dropped your pen, would you announce to yourself and anybody else who may be listening, "I'm going to try to pick this up?"

Words are real things and convey much to our own spirit and to others we are communicating with. Are you full of confidence, or wish washy and pusillanimous? How do you want to feel inside and be perceived from the outside? Living and flying through life with confidence and faith, purpose of action and deed, or living in timidity, fear, and indecision?

Which would you rather hear, and who would you fly with?

'I am going to try to land this plane.'

'I hope to land this plane.'

'I might land this plane.'

'I should be able to land this plane.'

'I think I can land this plane.'

'I believe I can land this plane.'

'I will land this plane.'

Many people use 'try' when they are looking for a gentle way to say they won't do it, or they are not sure. How much better would it be to be clear in our communications and say honestly what we really mean? 'I can't make a commitment now, but I'll get back to you,' or, 'I'm not sure, I will think about it.' Even saying 'no' and then offering if anything changes, to let someone know would be so much more respected. When we lie, or we are just unclear, it leaves us out of balance with ourselves and all others involved.

The way we feel about ourselves inside, and what we think others feel about us, has a great deal to do with our success. So, meaning what we say in integrity and commitment is extremely important to our well being.

The words we think and use all have meaning. 'Trying' would be on the bottom of any level of commitment and its use is normally an excuse, and is just plain setting ourselves up for failure.

Let's ban its use from our vocabulary and put our brain in gear before we let meaningless words flow out of our mouths and half-hearted actions dilute our effectiveness.

Why Shouldn't We?

'May your choices reflect your hopes, not your fears.'—Nelson Mandela

There are too many 'shoulds' running through our heads. In fact, most of us have been *shoulded* all over! It is time for a change! Whether it is the voice of our parents, the rules of proper society, or our moral conscience that is screaming in our inner ears, most time a 'should' comes flying at us, it is time to duck and take a look at its compunction. Let's find out what we really want, rather than letting the 'shoulds' blind programming push us into action.

How about taking the time to look at these *shoulds* when they pop up by examining the language of your thoughts? It is time to step back for a moment, every time these terrible shoulds come up. Stop and decide what is really best for you. Yes, many may be great ideas or actions, but rather than following blindly, be in your own choices and not of those terrible shoulds, directed by habit or others!

The Power of Prayer

'My prayer is gratitude. My intention is peace. My answer is Love.' – Anna Taylor

Rather than just continually asking for stuff, let's use our sharpened intention or prayers to create change and work miracles in our lives and that of others.

Prayer or intention, which some may rather call it, is one of the most powerful creative forces on our voyage here. As an aside, isn't it sad how many words or labels have been spoiled, in so many ways, by new associations or by being tied to corrupt religion or now despised religious practices?

It reminds me of the story of the atheist and an enlightened young student. The atheist was sharing in vociferous detail how he didn't believe in God. He was then asked to describe the god he didn't believe in and said: 'He is an all-powerful male being, whose sole purpose is to scare mankind into obedience with threats of punishment, hell, and damnation.' The student said, 'It is okay, I don't believe in that god either. He is nothing like mine!'

Prayer or intention is such a powerful creative force. Thoughts are things, and thought energy sent with *Love*, which is God, is probably the most powerful force in our world. Magnify that power, when two or more are agreed and sending that energy together mixed with belief, and miracles must ensue. Prayer or intention can change personal outcomes and even the course of nations!

It is little considered, but in the darkest days of World War II, just as the defeat of many men who were retreating caught against the wall of water in France was almost a certainty. Winston Churchill called the nation to prayer. The result: that day of prayer turned an almost certain defeat and enabled a rescue, which saved the lives of many, and in the longer term changed the tide of battle, which was eventually followed by victory. There are so many examples throughout history of weakness and seeming failure—then a turning through prayer, and finding the path back to victory.

There are many, both told and untold stories, where life has been changed forever, through prayer and intention. Use it—don't let its powers be stolen by the darkness of false associations and stolen beliefs.

Choose Empowering Beliefs

'Choose your thoughts wisely, for they are the energy that create your life.' —Author Unknown

Beliefs are neither true or false. They just are a collection of thoughts that have been thought so many times, they have become real to us.

Choose your thoughts.

Choose your feelings.

Some of the most basic barometers of how we feel and live our lives appear to work on set points. Just like the thermostat's temperature setting in our homes—once set, our levels of income, happiness, wealth and health— generally come back to the points that we are comfortable with, or that we have been programmed to accept.

What I found out, and many of us are realising is, with attention and focus, we can find the dial and reset any of these set points or levels of feeling.

It's strange, isn't it, that some of the poorest people in the world seem to have greatest levels of happiness?

You might ask how! Well, one of my carefully crafted and self-programmed beliefs is that, 'I am in control of my life, my feelings and every result that I get.' Thank you, Bob Proctor for a wonderful program. For thirty days, I thought and repeated that at every opportunity—now it is a part of my belief system.

Is it true in every situation? To be honest, I am not completely sure. However, I do know this: I have tried and tested it and used it in many situations, and I can attest, it has been one of my most empowering beliefs and has helped ease many a difficult experience. It has given me the feeling of control and certainty. This has proved so much more empowering than the opposite belief—that everything is out of my control, leaving only uncertainty, excuses and blame.

Tony Robbins shares that one of the basic needs of mankind is certainty!

Here is one of the main keys to the control panel, and thus flying this amazing machine. Believe you can! Then take control, choose, and write your own programmes!

You can change and update all of those preset levels of income, happiness, wealth, and health!

It's Time to Take Action! But How?

'True love is easy to find. Look in the mirror and love yourself, and love will shine on you forever.'—Author Unknown

From Louise Hay and Robert Holden's *'Life Loves You'* to Brian Tracey's suggestion to kiss the mirror and repeatedly say, 'I love you', the message and solutions are clear. It is time to reprogramme your spacecraft's very vocal warning and protection systems with a different set of empowering messages.

Sit in front of that mirror—a task that can be pretty hard, especially the first time. Look deep through the two windows of your craft, see that often shy and lonely creature within, and let your heart be filled with love and compassion. If led and you have never done any of this work before, you may want to wash those windows, so they can be sparkling clean and clear again—with a flood of tears from the nearby, so beneficial water ducts. You could even choose a deep heartfelt cry for the release from any of your old programmed thought patterns.

With time and repeated practice of more love and recognition in that mirror, the pilot within can become your best friend. That once neglected inner being can once again have light and joy shining from its eyes, becoming a glowing beacon of confidence and self-worth. It is becoming the kind of being that success can come out to meet. All those old voices are losing the power of the meaning—or was it the demeaning—you had previously given them. They are now fading into the oblivion of their own miserable past.

Life truly loves you! This becomes especially apparent, when you learn to *Love* yourself!

Take Action Anyway!

'Failure is only the opportunity to begin again, only this time more wisely.' – Henry Ford

Sometimes we genuinely can't tell where a particular line of thought or action will take us. You could trust that it wouldn't be a terminal decision and then ride it for a while to see what it could create or the direction it could lead. Go a bit further down that path and you will know. Or you could just decide to let it float on by. Another thought or idea of action will be sure to follow. Thus, you can avoid that creeping slow paralysis of indecision standing at the crossroads, like the poor bunny in the headlights and making no progress!

Are you too afraid of the consequences of the wrong choice? Why wait? We are here to experience! As many wise men have said, there is no such thing as failure, only lessons learnt on the journey. Even realising that was not the best choice, and learning what you don't want, can be useful information and a good lesson.

What Holds Us in the Darkness?

'You were born with wings, why prefer to crawl through life?'
— Rumi

Most of us awaken and journey through a world seemingly filled with darkness. However, this is the big illusion. Could it be that this chrysalis of darkness is the birthing place in our journey back into the light?

There is a great little book by Michael Mirdad entitled *'You are not going crazy. You are just waking up. The five stages of soul transformation process.'* We are, at core, all perfect beings. Our task is not to become perfect beings, it is to remember or wake up to that fact, and shed the cocoon of fears, false beliefs, and the clinging to the identity of our bitter experiences. Then we can enjoy this earthly journey instead of focusing on its struggles, blighted by the falsely programmed and impossible task of fixing things. Relax and let life flow, it will carry you to better places.

The caterpillar gets to a point where life, in that mode, is too much. Things crystallise and change. A struggle with the past, of the thick enclosure of the cocoon, is a needed part of the process. This struggle pumps life force and energy into all the parts of its new being: then the majestic butterfly emerges, shakes its incredible wings, and flies into the sunlight of a new day. It is beauty and freedom itself. The sunlight was always there. The promise or inner being of the butterfly was always there. It just had to pass through the dark night and the struggle of the ending of the old, into the birth of the new.

What Needs to Be Shed to Bring Us into the Light?

'Enlightenment is not a change into something better or more, but a simple recognition of who we truly already are.' – James Blanchard Cisneros

Our temporal world of illusion is made up of our beliefs, fears, and the habits we have accumulated, inherited or grabbed and clung on to. Paradoxically and strangely, these things have often been created for our 'safety!' The paradox is we are always perfectly safe. Nothing can harm the real being inside, the commander of our spacecraft, on this voyage through life. Yes, the illusion of our body can be harmed; however, even for this body, many documented miracles of healing and even life after death experiences show us that this craft can be totally renewed, regenerated, and healed. It just takes belief and can then happen—even sometimes in just an instant.

All things in this world are either based in *Love* or *fear*, which parallels *light* and *darkness*. Surely, it is time to shed those fears that hold us back in the darkness. The Bible repeats the magic truth 'Fear not' more than any other. This too is echoed in most words of truth, left for our guidance, by great teachers who have walked through this life before.

So what can we do? Recognise life loves us. Recognise, remember, and repeat, 'I am Love itself.' Do this until it becomes an unshakeable truth within your being. We must let go of the fears, lies, and false beliefs of inadequacy that keep us in the worlds of darkness.

Let us face the light and let its Love and the pull of its truths bring us into the knowledge of our true beings. Wake up, Children of Light. Your heritage and Divinity is within. We are just waiting for that perfect moment of remembering and the awakening into the joy of our true beings.

It's time for the 'What If Game.' – Review Questions

Here are the questions from the last section. Great questions lead to deeper answers. Let's take some time out to ponder on the answers that will come when you get quiet.

What could be the outcome if I adopted the belief 'I am responsible for my life, my feelings, and every result in my life?'

What if I learnt to ask great questions?

What if I started reprogramming my limiting beliefs with the opposite of those that hold me back?

What if I looked at all people through the eyes of acceptance and understanding?

What if all bitterness was replaced with forgiveness and Love?

What could be the resulting benefits if I stepped away from the regrets of the past and fears of the future?

What if I trusted life, and focussed on the desires I'd like to create?

What if feeding my mind and spirit became a higher priority in my life?

What if I carefully crafted positive thoughts to replace any that don't serve me any longer?

What if I have the desire to change, what is the commitment needed to make those changes and to make them stick?

What if my life could be cleansed from all that holds me back?

What would be the results if I used words of commitment and power in my thoughts and interaction with others?

What if I banished 'should' from my vocabulary and actions?

What if the power of prayer could change my world? What would I pray for?

What if I could change any of my preset levels of income, happiness, wealth and health? Which would I change first?

What if I took the time to learn how to love myself? What changes could I expect?

What if I just made that decision rather than procrastinating? What power would that bring?

What if life's struggles had a hidden purpose?

What if all fears and false illusions were to disappear? What would be left?

SECTION 4

Flying in Style

The Law of Attraction

'The Law of Attraction attracts to you everything you need, according to the nature of your thought life. Your environment and financial condition are the perfect reflection of your habitual thinking. Thought rules the world.' – Joseph Murphy

Make sure you have adjusted your programming to get all you really desire. Yes, we are all running, much of our time, on previous programming! Either the thought patterns, habits and programming that we have created ourselves, or those we accepted from others. These automatic programmes were created—mostly before we had enough wisdom to make informed choices for ourselves. Is it time to run through and inventory these mind programmes, to decide which serve us today? Awareness is a big part of the key! Mindfulness is great, that is, observing and being aware of what is going on with the thoughts in our heads. But, on a deeper level, what if those thoughts aren't taking us where we would like to go?

What we focus on expands! Strangely, this is why many people say *'The Secret'* and the Law of Attraction don't work. We often spend too long thinking about, or worse yet, talking about what we don't want—thus, as what we focus on expands, what we don't want will quickly be on its way into our reality.

If you want to change your world, focus on what you'd like and the qualities and things that you desire. I can't repeat it enough: *'What we focus on expands!'* Also, a bit of a paradox: don't want! As this is also—to an extent—a step to close to being desperate and an admission of lack. Focusing on lack—will also likewise lead to more lack!

There is a strange and different balance between desiring something and wanting something. Somehow, the laws that govern our universe seem to respond far better to desire and trust, rather than desperation and lack.

It works so much better to visualise and project your thoughts into the place of accomplishment of the desire, or the achievement of the dream. Stand in that place in your heart and mind, and feel the feelings of its success. Don't worry; it's not a lie, just a potential projection of your desired future. According to the Law of Attraction—and tried and proven results—this method of raising and entering into the vibration of your desire, as well as taking the steps that you can make towards it, is a sure-fire route towards manifestation.

One last caution: remember in this earthly realm, time rules. So be patient and trusting, rather than getting into the place of thinking it is not happening. This again would move things further away, and is also a key. Various different seeds, when sown, take different times to germinate, grow, and bring forth their fruit—thus, each desire or dream can take its own unknown time to manifest.

Just trust, have faith, and know deep inside, all you desire is, in due course, on its way!

Empowerment

'Decide today that you won't give up on your dreams and desires. Keep pressing forward, believing that you are anointed and empowered.' – Author Unknown

I am convinced—if we believe—that there are helpers, and the anointing to help with any task! We can be empowered to accomplish almost anything! Is the task you want to accomplish a mundane daily activity with a smile, or a challenging project? Or maybe it's leaping into an unknown dimension, outside of all previous experiences?

There is help at hand, both in the outer world from coaches, mentors, and those who have been that way before; or, if we get quiet and call for help, also from the host of spirit helpers, angels and guides, they are quite capable of sharing their wisdom and experiences by whispering into the inner parts of our understanding.

Just like there are books in libraries to give wisdom on most tasks, there can be heavenly helpers available for any task too. Check it out, just ask and believe!

What Will You Wear Today?

'It is your responsibility to make sure that positive emotions constitute the dominating influence of your mind.' – Napoleon Hill

A great way to start the day would be with a smile, an empowering thought, a little laugh, and a quick dose of gratitude. You can choose, but for a phenomenal day, I'd suggest that practice, either before, or just after you open your eyes.

Then the choice—yes, you can choose—what emotions would you like to wear now and every moment throughout the day? You may have forgotten how to make that choice—normally due to musty old habits that have attempted to creep in. They often arrived before you were really awake to your choices. But then—who would choose to keep wearing an old habit—unless you are planning on becoming a nun!

Our emotions are like clothes. We can choose what we wear! They are not us, or an integral part of our core being; they are choices we make that maybe have become habits. Now that can be great if they are good habits, those that you have chosen over time, but as things often degenerate, unless we are aware and work on them, many people are stuck or controlled by old habits and autopilot programmes.

Would you want to wear drab grey or angry red? That is not to categorise colours, but to show the choices we can make. Would you choose clothes that help you blend into the background—which most would not see? Are you afraid of your shadow or being noticed? Or would you choose, the bright vibrant colours of love, joy and compassion—to be glowing with happiness—that can melt and change your world, touching hearts and inspiring, lifting your own spirit and all the people you meet?

The Mystery of Money

'Money is neither my god nor my devil. It is a form of energy that tends to make us more of who we already are, whether it's greedy or loving.' – Dan Millman

More fears exist, and false limiting beliefs control us through our feelings about money, than almost any other fuel on our journey.

Money is not a piece of paper! It is almost just a value that we give ourselves, though it is much more! It's also the value we give things—ours, or others. They say: 'Calculate your net worth'. What a terrible way to value yourself!

Have you ever seen money? Yes, you have seen a wad of paper, a pile of coins, even a stack of gold bars, or the numbers on a bank statement, or on a cash point, or computer screen. These, however, again are not money, but just a perceived value or worth.

Money, like everything else, is energy! It almost doesn't exist in our physical plane, yet we can feel it, or especially we can feel it, when we perceive or believe that we don't have any, or can't get it; especially when that burning emptiness, desire, or desperation kicks in, when we feel we don't have enough for something we need or want.

Its value, or the value of the things we attach it to, is also constantly changing. Go abroad and your money is worth more, or less, when exchanged. Different things have quite different values in different countries. Each day your stocks, shares, gold, property, and other items of perceived worth, can be valued differently or in extreme cases, become worthless!

The Bible says, 'For the Love of money is the root of all evil.' Then it goes on to add a warning about coveting or desiring it too much, and the sorrows that can follow. Maybe the quote should translate to read, 'The excessive love of money.'

Actually, I'd suggest the best way to treat money is like a sensitive lover or a gentle dove. Don't hold it too tight or it will be gone! Don't lock it away and withhold it, or it will be of no use. It, like energy, works best and prospers most in flow.

Don't fear losing it or it will surely depart. Don't be too desperate or needy about it, or it will run away. Seek it, yes, and entice it with your best attitude, and faith along with a big smile, and it will come. Appreciate it and especially be grateful for the things, joys, and value it gives. Use it, give it, and share it! Play with it and share the joy with others and it will come back, stay, and multiply!

Have You Found Your Golden Goose?

'Success is doing what you want, when you want, where you want, with whom you want, as much as you want.' —Tony Robbins

Or have you ever dreamed of finding one? Or maybe, you don't even know what a Golden Goose is?

There is a story or fairytale of the farmer that found a goose. It laid a golden egg, every day. It brought him and his family, over time, great wealth. Very sadly, the story ends with a warning as he, or was it his wife, or maybe it was the mother-in-law, got greedy and wanted all the wealth at once, so they killed the golden goose to extract the gold. They couldn't find any inside, and so were left with nothing.

For me, the Golden Goose is the route to the Holy Grail of financial freedom, and thus eventually, financial abundance. Even more important for me is time and choice freedom— which financial freedom brings. That freedom is the knowing that all bills and expenses are covered each month before going to work, or play, with an ongoing, regular, and secure stream of income.

After some years of working towards this as a dream and goal, I have achieved it. It's not great wealth or huge abundance yet, though for me, that freedom of choice and security is great wealth and abundance. This also brings the knowledge that even more wealth will follow.

It's a sad fact that most people are living in a situation where, if they were unable to work, or lost their job, they would lose their homes and livelihoods within months or at best, have to survive on the minimal and rapidly decreasing government subsistence. How long would it be for you, if your work suddenly dried up or you were made redundant or hospitalised? Do you have a plan in place or sufficient income for the lifestyle you'd expect upon retirement—or are you planning on working until you fall into an early grave?

How does the alternative of finding your Golden Goose feel now? Could it be worth the hunt and effort? There are many potential routes to that financial freedom and entire books written on the subject. These are well worth investigating; in the meantime, I will share a few ideas to get you started, along with some things that have worked for me.

One of the biggest lessons is to make a start and accumulate some extra money to invest, or even get out of crippling debts. To do this, you need to cut unnecessary expenses. It is a strange paradigm that most people, no matter what their incomes, spend all of that money every month. Lots of people also spend even more than their incomes. It takes accessing what is really needed and looking for ways to cut the extra fat so it can be turned into golden eggs—wise investments—for the future. It's amazing that even saving one pound or dollar a day, is seven in a week, thirty in a month, and 365 in a year. Many of us could quite easily claw back from the fat, far more than just one pound or a dollar a day. Wise investments, compounded over time, can produce great flows of wealth. This can especially work well for those who are wise enough to adopt this strategy at an early age.

For those of you who can't find or don't have that extra money, there is another magic ingredient that can be invested. Your time! Can you trim the fat out of that, or more wisely invest parts of it, to turn it into a Golden Egg producing asset? Many people say they just don't have time. Are you one? Actually, time usage is all about priorities and values. We all have the same amount of time each day. Some people have just discovered how to value and leverage their time to greater effect. In that process, they have discovered many ways to create wealth.

Most people are stuck in the commonly taught and programmed routine of exchanging basic time for basic money. Again, for many people, that is very basic money or just subsistence. Even people, who have figured out how to create more value and thus more money for their time, are still stuck just exchanging time for money. If that time was interrupted, they too would be unstuck—that is, if anything happened to their ability to provide their time.

There is a better way! Though most haven't considered or been prepared to make the adjustments and efforts needed to realise it. How about exchanging a little regular time to create your golden goose? It's amazing how many solutions can be discovered and applied when deciding to do this.

There are some great MLM or network marketing opportunities available where investing time can create leverage. This works by helping others to also succeed and create a true residual income. Beware though and make wise choices, as some, in seeking to jump on the bandwagon, over promise and under deliver. Some too, with flawed plans and poor compensation packages, soon fail. Fortunately, I was led to a great one that has brought me—along with other actions and learning's over time—to the excellent position of financial freedom. There are many great and excellent companies to choose from worldwide. With some research, personal growth and effort, if this is the direction that is right for you, I am sure you could find something that can work, if you are prepared to work at it!

Or maybe you could write a best-selling book, or pop song, improve or invest in property, add value to some items and sell them, or share your knowledge through membership sites or manuals, etc.

From an ethical point, beware of schemes that don't add value and just seem to be created to take from others. Some trading or currency schemes seem to be just about scooping money out of the markets without giving any value—many are extremely risky, and cannot be sustained—especially when all personal gains are at the result of the expense and losses of others.

In all your endeavours, remember the Golden Rule. Whatever you do, do it in *Love* and with consideration for others—Win-Win! Then the Dream and Goal, the Holy Grail of Financial Freedom, will be on its way. You will find it is worth all the growth, labour and testing you will experience en route to that achievement.

It brings to mind one of Jim Rohn's famous teachings: 'Seek to become a millionaire, not for the money, but for the lessons along the way. In achieving that million, you will become a millionaire person and should that million flee or be taken away, it will soon return.'

There are many Golden Geese out there, available for anyone who is sincerely seeking in honesty and integrity. I wish you the best in finding yours.

The Pursuit of Happiness

'Happiness does not depend on what you have or who you are; it solely relies on what you think.' – Buddha

King Solomon was offered his choice of qualities and he chose wisdom. Then all other things were added unto him!

Too many people seem to be stuck in a relentless pursuit of wealth, thus acknowledging they haven't got it. They think it will bring them happiness. Yes, it can go a long way to help, and it is okay to play that game. However, first—just maybe— learning to be happy in whatever state we are in could bring the start of a higher and more fulfilling way. Then all things and wisdom could be free to help us to really take off and fly in this wondrous playground of life. Could it be all it takes, is to realise how wonderfully wealthy we already are?

Happiness is not something we just get by actions or possessions, but something we choose! Our happiness level can be full, regardless of exterior situations. Like the old question, which comes first: the chicken or the egg? I'd say happiness comes first, and then we can experience the golden eggs of life.

Maybe we are taking this whole journey or game of life too seriously? What if the main points were scored by positively touching our own and other's lives—thus increasing our own and other's happiness levels—and living a full and exciting life?

Who made the rules and wrote the programmes we have been flying with? Most, it seems, were written by our ancestors, designed for our protection, in a different age or by well-meaning parents teaching what they knew or had been taught themselves, for their protection as children. Or maybe we were programmed by our churches or religions, seeking to keep us on their way or their particularly narrow route, into their ideas of heaven, more to control us, than set us free; thus making sure we stay under their influence and contribute to support their missions through dogmas, and the fear of eternal damnations. Maybe they want us to be miserable here, so we seek their route to salvation, rather than enjoying the journey of this life here and now.

Sex, Nudity, Freedom, and the Divine

'If we were meant to be nude, we would have been born that way.' – Oscar Wilde

Your gleaming beautiful spacecraft has millions of dedicated pleasure sensors. It has entire systems designed to release more powerful feel good drugs than anything that can be purchased illegally. It can take you to places of divine bliss, with energy, light and orgasm, rippling through every cell. It arrives in this universe naked in its wondrous beauty. It can provide some of the most beautiful experiences of connection with other voyagers.

Yet these systems, controls, and gauges, are plagued with more false limiting programming than probably any of the other areas of command and control in our lives.

Fears, guilt, and jealousies wreak havoc on most being's voyages; and spoil, or limit many of the pleasures and experiences that, I believe, our wonderful crafts are designed to fly us through. The opportunity for heavenly bliss and connection is inbuilt, yet in so many cases, we have been sold short and end up with a quick spurt of limited sensation.

It's been said the devil hates sex, but loves to promote it! The media and advertising are full of the power of sex, yet that conformity programmes shout, 'don't you dare to show too much interest in it, or you are a weird, promiscuous, sex maniac, or pervert.' Why is it that the natural, physical things of connection and love are considered more obscene than hatred, war and violence?

How did these things start? How many limiting beliefs and fears have been impounded into our consciousness? In many cases, these were by well-meaning parents seeking to protect us; in others, by religions and governments seeking to control us. Did it start in infancy with, 'You shouldn't touch that bit?' Or 'Cover that up, it's naughty!' Or was it the religious teachings that claim sex is only for procreation and shouldn't be enjoyed? Maybe it was the old wives' tales, which share that men are evil creatures that just want to take advantage of you. Or possibly, current fears of loss if another being was to see or enjoy the beauty of your partner. Maybe you can think of other fears or beliefs that stifle your own pleasures?

Who first taught us that some parts of our bodies were more taboo than others? Why, in some ages, was it considered too revealing to see an ankle? Yet now, sometimes, all is revealed. How come it's okay to kiss a cheek, but too risky to kiss on the lips? Yet in other situations or cultures, it could be considered unfriendly not to? Why is it considered okay by most people to touch an arm, but improper to touch a breast? It's okay to pay for a massage, but whoa, a massage to touch and pleasure our most sacred bits could be considered immoral and illegal.

Yes, set your boundaries and live with them, but be careful they don't become chains that destroy the experiences and pleasures that are a part of the functions of our incredible crafts. Especially, make sure that they are the boundaries of your choice, and not some arbitrary blockages programmed by others for a different age or situation and held in by the fears and the penalties thus imposed.

It was the Divine that created your beautiful body and filled it with so many pleasure sensors that it's almost impossible to count them. So enjoy it, and all the pleasures and love it can bring. Life Loves You!

Forgiveness Is Loving Ourselves!

'Forgiveness is not always easy. At times, it feels more painful than the wound we suffered to forgive the one that inflicted it. And yet, there is no peace without forgiveness.' Marianne Williamson

It has been said that forgiveness is the perfume a beautiful flower leaves on the heel that crushed it. Consider that gift of forgiveness. It is a blessing, in spite of all the hurt, which has to come from a source far greater than our human ego! I believe each of us has that place of Divine love within and can, if we choose, reach it.

I used to feel that forgiveness should only be applied when I was asked in a humble way by the offender for that forgiveness, and sadly, would then often only bestow it in an unfeeling, compassionless and self-righteous way. Lord, forgive me!

If you were to hold onto that belief, things would come unstuck if the person concerned was to pass away or never see you again. Is it worth a life with that root of bitterness burning away, causing problems in the whole of you? It's a strange thing and could seem an injustice, but the only person that resentment and hurt is harming is our self! In fact, the other offence would have triumphed, causing an unrepaired hurt. So by the same reasoning, the gift of forgiveness is going to be the bigger cleansing to ourselves, although I am sure by universal laws, it does also affect the one it is directed to, especially where it can be done in person or with a direct message.

Someone has said that the ultimate revenge is forgiveness. I would prefer to believe the ultimate cleansing is forgiveness, as it is almost certainly only our human experience and ego that would want us to get even with another.

When we realise that we have, in some way or another—even just in the depth of thought—committed the same or similar hurts, then that acknowledgement and its own cleansing by self-forgiveness, gives us the Love to forgive all others. In fact, everything boils down deep inside, to the greater difficulty, and most important task of loving and forgiving ourselves.

Take some time in the beauty of your heart that special place of Love, where all forgiveness of self and others flows—bathe in its balm, enjoy the perfume of a thousand flowers that can be found there; relax, let all past hurts be washed and cleansed with the powerful prayer. 'I'm sorry, please forgive me. Thank you, I love you.' It works for you, it works for others, and even the atrocities in your world can be cleansed. Use it and see, over time, how everything and anything can be healed and cleansed.

Are You Planning Your Life?

'A dream becomes a reality as a result of your actions, and your actions are controlled to a large extent by your habits.' – John C. Maxwell

How long have you spent planning a holiday? Thinking about and researching what you might see and visit, checking out hotels, working out the flights or travel times and costs; maybe getting a guidebook or spending time on Trip Advisor checking out all the best ways to experience or enjoy your trip; changing currency, maybe even learning a few words of another language, and so on?

So, what have you done in planning, and have you thought about how you would like your life to turn out? Do you even realise you can plan it? Thoughts create things; so conversely, the lack of thought will mean you are stuck, drifting along, rudderless and often headed round and round in meaningless circles and slowly sinking. That way too, you will find others will have planned your life or are controlling it—then most of the time it works out for their advantage, not yours.

It's time to take a stand! First, believe that you can and then take some time out and decide what kind of life would be your ideal? Consider if money and time were not limiting, what would you like to do, to be and to have? If you believe it and invest time in creating it in your heart and thoughts, 'All things are possible to him or her that believes.' Don't be afraid to dream! The master plan for our voyage here, it is for our enjoyment, not drudgery, poverty and pain, or even just shades of the same.

Run movies in your head and the feelings in your heart of possessing your ideals and dreams. It's probably best to aim to create one thing, or work on one area at a time. Maybe life will magically change your present circumstances and fill them with light, a raise, and harmony; instead of discord with those closest, more time for you and the experiences you desire, or maybe there will be a complete change of scenery and lifestyle. Be open to both, sow the seeds of desire and water them carefully. Feed them by living them inside and feeling their fulfilment—in due time they will be manifested outside in your world.

Past Lives or Seeing Through the Eyes of Others that Have Been Before?

'Life is a school, where you learn how to remember what your soul already knows.' – Author Unknown

Is there even a difference? The collective being, which is the mind, energy and spirit that empowers us all, has observed many human experiences throughout the ages of this earth. Was it actually us or me that experienced these events? And for the sake of argument, what is 'me,' or 'us' anyway, when thinking on that level? And again, does it matter? There are definitely amazing experiences to view or remember, sometimes in incredible detail. Whether they were yours or that of a spirit guide with whom you are inextricably linked, does it matter?

It sure wasn't the same spacecraft/body that you are flying in now, but then, that isn't the same craft you were flying just seven years ago, as every cell in its physical being is known to have changed in that time. Is it really important or possible to understand with our minds all the incredible mysteries of Spirit? Let's just enjoy and explore all these wonderful experiences, and thus ponder.

Do You Desire a Soul Mate?

'Love is our true destiny. We do not find the meaning of life by ourselves alone – we find it with another.' – Thomas Merton

This is a huge desire burning in the hearts of many alone or lonely people. Sometimes, this pull is stronger and at other times, walls and protections have been built against it, often caused by previously wounded hearts. Many people have given up—adopting beliefs that this is not for me, or maybe all the good ones are gone. Yet so frequently, there remains a calling—deep in the heart—that desire for a special intimate connection.

I am in the fortunate and blessed position of having walked a way along that long journey of growth, and manifested a beautiful soul mate. Love at first sight, or was it just the knowing of two divine beautiful souls—connecting and seeing a shared destiny in the depths of each other's eyes?

Beautiful, yes, but amidst these early passions and the message of hope that this is possible—I must also share a warning. This is just the first step of a journey together that can become more like—two rough boulders hewn from the mountain and tumbling together into a tempestuous cauldron, in a corner of the turbulent ocean.

We have learnt the lessons of oneness—or was it aloneness—and now come the greater lessons of togetherness.

Bound together by attraction and commitment in the ocean—at times it rages, and the two boulders frequently grind together, knocking all the rough edges from each other. Eventually, in an undetermined time, smooth pebbles are emerging, having peeled off many layers and past hurts, reaching a core of tenderness and Love.

When one submits to this process, it can become a treasure house of some of life's greatest lessons and growth. Sadly, I feel too many of us can run screaming in a state of blame, rather than realising all the things that we see without are merely reflections of our inner thoughts and beings, which, when we submit and love ourselves and the others involved, can become huge steps of growth in life's school and learning processes.

Well, after the warning on the cigarette package—we can get around to enjoying the experience. I must say the journey is not just about the tough moments of growth—it can be, most especially, about the many beautiful moments of connection, empathy, and the shared pleasures of *Love* creating and *Love* making.

Some Tips and Ideas Experienced from My Soul Mate Manifestation Process

'As you awaken, you will come to understand that the journey to love isn't about finding 'the one', it's about becoming 'the one'.' – Creig Crippen

It is not all about finding the perfect soul mate; in fact, he or she will be just as imperfect as you believe you are. So how about looking to become more like the one that your ideal soul mate would desire?

Yes, make your list of what you would like in your soul mate, though realise the journey and the quest can often be more about realising what you don't like.

Don't narrow your search too much. Be open to the surprise of realising your prospective soul mate could, in many areas, be a diametric opposite of what you think. If each of you were narrowing your search too much, especially in the new age of Internet dating, the odds of ever meeting would be shrinking into nonexistence.

I don't believe there is just one potential soul mate. There are thousands out there. Remember though, that even sometimes, when finding one of these soul mates, they may not be at the right time or place in their lives to be able to make any further or deeper connection work.

We can easily get so set on exterior characteristics, that we forget that which our heart desires is another compatible heart.

Watch out about limiting by age. Many people's true age does not match their supposed earth life years in wisdom or experiences. Some are still young, yet are wise in experience. Some are old and closed in habit and outlook. Others are full of life and desire, whilst many have gone to sleep and left their engines barely running. Which are you?

Again, like most things on our journey, it is all about beliefs. These are the things that are sculpting your existence and everything that manifests in your exterior world. Are some of these thoughts running through your head? 'I will never find the one.' 'All the good ones are gone.' 'It is not worth the struggle.' 'I'm not worthy, how could anyone love me?' Maybe it is time to change your thoughts?

Again, the most important step in finding and keeping the *Love*—and in fact everything you desire—is to *Love* yourself! So working through that journey, clearing and cleansing all self-hating and limiting beliefs, is the prime step in finding and keeping all the experiences you desire.

Integrity—Live in Truth

'Integrity is doing the right thing even when no one else is watching.' – C. S. Lewis

Jim Rohn taught entire classes on Integrity. I would highly recommend searching out his teachings. One of my favourite lessons that he shared is not to be seeking success, but become the person success comes to find. To become that person, it is vital to realise that we need to walk in integrity and build character. These are crucial components of lasting success!

Strangely, integrity isn't only about how we treat others. One of the worst people you can lie to or let down is yourself—after all, you have to live with yourself 24/7! If we are in inner conflict and lacking in self-respect or self-love, we will have already been defeated in all genuine attempts to win hearts and influence others and live a life of integrity. People sense our own feelings about ourselves and they treat us accordingly. So lying, cheating, or even just being half-hearted is the quickest way to self-defeat.

All of these things can be the beginning of the slippery slope into a pit of self-hatred or despair. Fortunately though, as they say, 'while there is life, there is hope.' One decision, like in Jim Rohn's story, 'The day that turned my life around,' can turn us back on the road to a life of Love and self-respect, changing how we think about ourselves, our inner vibration, and thus how others perceive us.

In Jim Rohn's case, he had reached a point of broke desperation, compounded by lying to a girl scout whom he would like to have helped, but had no money to afford even a few pennies for some cookies. What will it take to turn your life around? Or maybe it was something that happened years ago that propelled you in a new direction?

It takes creating time for growth, and also consistent practice and concerted effort to continue in the right direction. However, the miracle of a change of thought, which can be just a decision, is all that is needed to make a start.

I Am

'Anytime you start a sentence with 'I AM' you are creating what you are and what you want to be.' – Wayne Dyer

I am! This is one of the most powerful statements in the universe—for God is the Great I Am.

Sadly for decades, many of us have misused this command and attached many negative values and meanings to our "I am' statements." Thus, we have created many of the weaknesses and faults that we see ourselves as having. Thoughts create things, and what we focus on expands.

Consider which of these 'I am' statements—or maybe I should say commands—you are repeating every day, sometimes, even hundreds of times.

Is it:

'I am fat, thin or even ugly?'

'I am stupid!'

'I am forgetful!'

'I am broke!'

'I am clumsy!'

'I am sick!'

'I can't' is almost as powerful!

How about replacing these limiting commands with positive affirmations? It may take a while and repeated practice, but just consider how your world might change if all or many of the following commands were firmly installed in your belief systems.

'I am loved!'

'I am beautiful!'

'I am powerful!'

'I am successful!'

'I am wealthy!'

'I am strong!'

'I am healthy!'

Take a look at your life and see how many 'I Am's' it would benefit you to replace? Use what you desire to become, and not the limiting thoughts that you may have been imprisoning yourself in.

Tip: You could review and then write down all the similar statements you make. Then in that list, cross out the ones that don't empower, writing next to them the opposite of your previous disempowering commands. Then, take time to work to change your habitual thoughts and automatic programmes to match and grow your new desired realities.

For Those Suffering Loss

'Goodbyes are only for those who love with their eyes. Because for those who love with heart and soul, there is no such thing as separation.'—Rumi

When the cleansing tears have slowed, or there is a break from the questioning mind, take a moment to enter the quiet place in the centre of your beautiful heart. Ask for the grace to see the picture, hear the message, or feel the feelings from the other side.

If it is a loved one you have lost, look at their face, feel their presence, and ask how they would like you to feel—would they really want you to bear the burden of such sadness, especially if you could see and understand the beautiful place, the calling, the new experiences and vision that they now have? Hear their promise and take comfort in their smile. In spite of all past hurts, they love you. It was just time to journey on.

Know that, though it seems realms away, through walls created by forgetfulness and senses almost lost in the past— the place where we all abide is only a thin veil away. In that special place, that quiet place in the temple of your heart, you can connect through that veil and know all is well. It is a part of a beautiful plan that was agreed in a time before.

There is growth for all and understandings to come before the time of knowing and no more tears. For now, trust and accept their blessings. Look with joy at all you have—the past pleasures and shared experiences. Don't dwell on perceived losses and especially not on imagined losses, or fears for your loved one, or for your future. If you could see even a glimpse of all they would tell, you would feel such happiness for them—life's heaviness and burdens all left behind.

As you leave that quiet place, take a moment to realise that *'Life Loves You'* too. There can be beauty even in great loss and new beginnings. Life is waiting to show you its smile—when you are ready to receive it. Take a look. The sun always eventually comes out from behind the dark storm clouds. That storm having washed and cleansed the earth. What new life would you like to create? Believe everything and anything is possible. Healing can be in a moment. Is there real benefit in dwelling on loss? Make the most of all you have left. Could it be now time to look for the silver lining, that rainbow at the end of the storm? It is always there—when you can believe.

It's time for the 'What If Game.' – Review Questions

Here are some more 'What If' questions from each of the topics before. Would it be okay to take the time to play with your answers and thoughts on these questions? The answers you receive will help compound your learnings and make pathways for growth.

You could also come and join our community on Facebook; it is a private group for people who have read this book. You will need to request to join before seeing the content. You will find us at www.Facebook.com/groups/FlyBacktoLove. It is a great place to share your answers, lessons, ideas and growth from the principles in the book. You can also ask for, or give support.

What if, with the right attitude, the Law of Attraction works? What would I attract into my life?

What if the power and help was available to accomplish any task, reach any desire, or achieve any dream—what would I choose?

What if I developed the habit of consciously choosing my emotions before stepping into each day or situation?

What if my attitude to money could change? How could I best think about it and use it?

What if financial freedom was possible for me? Would I be prepared to pay the price and make the commitment to create it?

What would it feel like if I were freed from all taboos and fears about my divine being and all the pleasures it was created to enjoy?

What if forgiving another healed me? Would I be prepared to forgive them and myself?

What if I could see the results of spending time planning my life? Where would I like to be headed? What would I like to achieve?

What if I enjoy this wonderful journey, instead of spending too much effort analysing the details?

What if I could both learn and love in my journey, seeking connection with others?

What would be the result if I spent more attention becoming the one, rather than seeking the one?

What it I spent some time replacing negative thoughts with positive affirmations, creating beliefs in line with all I desire?

What if I focussed on being true to myself?

What if the 'I Am' statement became a powerhouse of growth for me?

What if I could see clearly beyond the loss, and celebrate life and a connected future with the one who has passed on?

SECTION 5

Fly Back to Love

Reaching Your Idea of Heaven Is Not the Goal—It's Enjoying the Journey!

'So often we become so focussed on the finish line that we fail to enjoy the journey.' – Dieter F. Uchtdorf

Too many of us fly through life, chasing the elusive butterfly of success. I know—I was an expert at it! The trouble is that we never catch it, or even if it appears we do for a few seconds, then it's soon off again. So then the chase is on again, for the next achievement, goal, or promotion. Leaving behind burnt earth in a parched land is often the result of such relentless pursuit! We eventually burn out ourselves, and also often those closest to us—that is if they didn't flee a long time before.

At one point, I realised this was just what I had been doing for many years. Yes, I had been reaching many of my goals, but then constantly rushing towards the next—never taking time to breathe, pause, and smell that sweet essence of success. Wouldn't it be great to celebrate the victory with those closest to us and then rest for a while before shooting off towards the next mountain peak?

After one session of somewhat painful and relentless soul searching, I realised much of this was caused by my own insecurities and poor self-worth. I'd felt I had to prove to those around me that I was worthy of their love, appreciation, and respect. This was especially true of my relationship with my father. For years, as a child, I had felt such a failure. I had missed so much of all he desired that I would become. It's sad to realise that his driving force was probably down to similar programming as a child. Such harsh expectation-led drive, rather than bathing in unconditional love, was for years the norm. This common method of child rearing must have scarred and left many lonely, unhappy children. Within the core being of many, even the greatest achievers, there is often such a sad, lonely, insecure child, still hoping and looking for Love.

This is just one example of the way our spacecraft has been programmed. To take control of our own spacecraft and help the next generations of earth explorers, it's time to change that code and replace it with much more meaningful values and flight instructions.

In our relentless pursuit of success, it's too easy to forget what life is really about! Surely, it's the collection of our experiences and the memorable moments that count! Remembering too, Love and happiness gauges that measure full most of the time—no matter what the circumstances or situation we find ourselves in. That, in my manual, is where it's at! How about yours?

One of Jim Rohn's great teachings was to become a millionaire, not for the million, but for the lessons learnt along the way; and then, even if you lose the million, you will have become a millionaire person and that million will soon come back to you! Let's take the time to enjoy this wonderful journey of Life.

An Adventure in Goal Setting

'Life will only change when you become more committed to your dreams than you are to your comfort zone.' – Billy Cox

Before any journey as in life, there comes a time when we must decide where we want to go, or what we want to achieve. Just imagine, you are a ship's captain and it's time to set out on a voyage, which would work best? 'Crew, we're off on this journey, let's just push the boat out and see where we end up?' Or, 'Crew, we are off to explore a new land. I have plotted a course that we can adjust en route as needed, but for now, we are headed Southeast towards the setting sun. Pull up the anchor and let's go.'

In the first case, the ship would float out and be pushed by whatever winds arose. It would probably go round in circles and in the worst case, crash into some rocks and sink; or maybe, eventually just drift back to where it had started, accomplishing nothing!

This is like life! Unless we have a purpose and a reason that some call our 'Why', which helps us set a direction, then our life frequently just drifts in mediocrity. I listened to a great thought leader, Randy Gage, who described mediocrity as the opposite of success. Too many people seem afraid of failure and describe it as the opposite of success. If only we could all believe that failure is just one, or maybe many, of the steps towards success?

There are two methods of goal setting. Some teachers share that you should always set goals in the SMART way. That's Specific, Measurable, Attainable, Realistic and Timed. This type of goal is planned in detail, clearly seen and achievable, with every step thought through by imagining the result, then stepping back through the process to plan all the actions required.

Other people say we should set big, hairy, audacious goals, which push the very boundaries of belief. When successful, they can take us to places almost beyond the seemingly possible—maybe up that steep mountain to the pinnacles of success. This is the type you put on a piece of paper or a vision board and almost forget about, until one day, when you discover it's been achieved. I think there is a place for both.

One of the way goals work is using an amazing part of our brain called the reticular activation system—RAS for short. Did you ever buy a new car and when first driving it, suddenly see lots of the same type and colour cars everywhere? This is that system at work. We see what we are looking for!

Buzzing around in the huge energy field of life are trillions of bits of information—but the poor, limited, conscious mind can only cope with so much without exploding. So this RAS saves us from too much information and filters down what we see, so that we only experience what we focus on. This takes us to another truth that is very important in goal setting. Thoughts create things!

The most important step is first deciding what we really desire, and then by default what we are willing to give up to attain those desires. Randy shared that we have to make that decision, or else make the decision to give up on those dreams, and remain stuck inside our comfort zones.

The comfort zone is a bit like a fish bowl. We frequently end up swimming round in ever decreasing circles as we grow that bit larger, and yet we are still afraid to break that thin glass wall that only lets us see glimpses of the great ocean. Wouldn't it be sad to miss the wonders of that ocean, the many fish to swim with, and exploring the majesty of freedom and all life's wonderful possibilities?

Have you decided on or taken time to listen to Spirit and discover your purpose? Have you laid some plans, the course, and direction for how you can attain this grand vision or souls calling? It's never too late!

Did you know that some spacecraft, before the longest journeys, have to circle the earth a few times, building power over the gravity—that has seemingly held them trapped—then using its force as a slingshot to catapult them forward, escaping its constant pull, and moving them rapidly onwards towards their exciting goals?

So even now, if you feel stuck just circling the earth—know that there are available, hidden powers to reach any goal. Maybe there are just a few more of life's lessons to learn before starting your journey? It is sometimes those lessons, which may seem curses at the time, but yet give us the breaking or determination, and thus the strength, and the push to go on to our true desires and destiny. After all, why settle for mediocrity when there are the true oceans of life and success to explore and experience?

As evidenced by many that have attained their dreams, you are never too old, or too young, and there are almost no limits to the diversity of goals, desires, and dreams that can be attained. It just takes that desire, mixed with energy and direction, and the willingness to blast off, leave the comfortable earth behind and fly towards your dreams.

If you haven't yet done so, take the time soon to get quiet and take the first steps of the choice. Ask yourself—if I could do, be or have anything, what would it be? And then, what am I prepared to give up to achieve this?

Have You Created a Vision Board?

'If you can dream it, you can do it.' – Walt Disney

A vision board is a great way to speed the manifestation process. For those who may not know, it is usually a collection of pictures encapsulating your goals and desires. It is normally kept somewhere that is frequently visible—it can help and speed the process of bringing your dreams into your reality. Sometimes, even the actions of creating one can jump-start the magic process of manifestation. Remember, 'Thoughts create things' and 'We see what we are looking for.' When you are clear on what you would like to create, I would highly recommend taking the time to make one.

I had an exciting experience creating and living one. On New Year's Day, a group of about forty people were in a New Year's workshop and taking the time to create our own vision boards for the year. Time was running out and two last pictures came to mind. I decided I would like to find and add a picture of the Great Wall of China. I had thought of travelling there one day, and also, a picture of a book—to bring further into my reality the book that I felt wanted to be born. I approached the table with a stack of magazines where there were still a few people hurriedly leafing through pages, searching for their desired pictures. Amazingly, as a beautiful sign, I picked up the first magazine and flipped it open and there was a picture of the Great Wall, with the caption 'Explore New Places.' I thought, 'Wow!' 'So where is my book?' And the very next page I flipped open, there was the picture—actually of three books!

The trip to China materialised and was amazing. It also happened months before I thought possible, in April, and it worked out for far less than such a trip would normally cost. Then along came an email from Hay House, advertising their writer's workshop in May. Subsequently, whilst attending it, I made the firm my commitment to make the book happen.

Now a few months later, the book's writing stage is close to completion. A vision board, mixed with intention, has magical powers!

Avoid wanting things too much, as this becomes almost a dwelling on the lack of them. It is the intention of desire and the knowing, that they are there already in your confident future that your treasured desires have already been created and are just awaiting the perfect time for you to step into them. This is what brings them smoothly into being!

When you have done all of the smaller steps to prepare, create in thought, and be ready, then the Universe and your Higher Self will see you mean business, and the flow will begin. The treasures of your tomorrow are waiting to be created in your beautiful heart and thoughts today.

How Do You See the World?

'Sanity may be madness, but the maddest of all is to see life as it is not as it should be.' —Don Quixote

I'm convinced that we all have choices and what we choose to visualise and see, in time, creates our reality. We can choose to live in routine mediocrity or create through thoughts and our beliefs—which are merely repeated thoughts—our dream worlds.

Have you seen the movie 'Man of La Mancha,' the story of Don Quixote, with Peter O'Toole and Sophia Loren? If not, maybe you have heard the song, from the movie, 'To Dream the Impossible Dream.'

Take some time to search out and read or listen to the words from this song on the Internet. It is truly envisioning and inspiring—a message with a sincere heart cry and a picture of the journey of awakening. Unfortunately, I was unable to get permission to reproduce them here.

Don Quixote lived in a different world than the bleak world of most of the normal folks of his time. It was the time of the Spanish Inquisition when people departing even slightly from what was considered the true faith, or ways to behave would suffer torture, imprisonment, or death. He was considered insane by all around him, with well-meaning relatives attempting all they could to turn him from his quest, which they perceived as insanity. He was on a personal crusade to right all wrongs and change his world. He fought giants, which most people perceived as windmills.

He fell in love with, defended, and fought for a local prostitute and barmaid, Aldonza, calling her 'His Lady, Dulcinea.' He was supported by his squire Sancho Panza, who rode a donkey, and who was constantly bemused by his beloved master's antics.

Amazingly, he eventually won the heart of Dulcinea, after almost being killed defending her. After many adventures and tussles with evil, he fell sick. Fortunately, Dulcinea finally also caught his vision of a better world. She then joined the ever-faithful Sancho Panza to carry on his vision and crusade. A life changed by *Love*!

This is such a beautiful parable. If we can believe and live our vision, with passion and persistence, in spite of all the world throws at us, what changes may be accomplished and hearts won!

The Ramblings of a Mad Man

'There is no great genius without some touch of madness.' – Seneca

I was asked to talk about mad scientists, and realised there is such a narrow gap, if any, between what is commonly accepted as genius and insanity. Who is to say what the difference is?

Most pioneers, visionaries, world changers and prophets, have at first been considered insane by the masses—at least until their invention, discovery, or warning became manifest. Their completely different lifestyles, ideas and results have explored places that normal people would fear to go. They share ideas that in many cases challenge common beliefs and the status quo. They have flown their spacecrafts directly opposite to known routes and common programmes, and kept the world from solidifying into the mindless, stuck sludge of conformity. To hell with the proper way!

Perfect Peace in the Midst of a Storm

'Perfect peace isn't dependent on perfect circumstances. It comes from a steadfast, trusting heart.' – Amy Carroll

'Thou will keep him in Perfect Peace whose Mind is stayed on Thee.' This is a beautiful verse and solution from the Bible, but what is Perfect Peace and how can we rest in it?

Someone once shared that the best picture of peace was not a beautiful harmonious pastoral scene, but a picture of peace, in the midst of a storm. Imagine a beautiful bird singing on a branch next to her young baby birds in their nest, which is perched high above a raging cataract, a roaring torrent of water pouring through the rocky chasm below, splashing very close to that nest, but never harming it or her precious young, as a dark thunderous storm, flashing with lightening is just leaving. That little bird has faith. She knew her nest was out of the reach of life's storms—even though so close to the midst of them.

How about us? When is it our faith gets tested? What triggers us the most, and threatens to steal our peace? And how can we avoid losing it? What is the solution? Whether it is an inner storm of anger, or upset, or an outer storm of disturbing and threatening circumstances—there is always peace that can be found!

Well, I know what it's not, and doesn't work! Panic or a hissing fit of anger or hurt, would be great to write off the list. When the storm comes and it's not possible to fix it, then the way to live in that moment, and the essence of peace, is maintaining an inner knowing that in spite of the seeming circumstance, all is well and will turn out well. In fact, knowing and believing that all that unfolds is a part of life's beautiful and ever perfect plan—this is what brings peace.

It's too easy to look at the waves and the raging storms of circumstances. Remember: 'what we focus on expands,' so by nature, things will get worse and worse whilst we focus on the problem. The sooner we can make that stand in our heart of hearts, and let the feeling and knowing that all is well wash over us and then hold onto it so tight, in faith that no fears can enter in, the quicker and stronger that perfect peace can be maintained or return. When it boils down to it, in such dire circumstances—what can we actually do anyway—so why not trust Love and watch the fears flee? Or in an inner storm, stop, and get quiet. Standing still in your beautiful heart centre can usually also still the raging ego, or the ranting of your wounded child, or any other part of you that appears to be throwing a fit in that moment.

Again, it boils down to the wonderful equation and empowering truth—that there only exists a state of Love or fear. I know from past bitter experiences which choice pays dividends. Which would you desire to choose in every circumstance? Even at the end of this life, all fears can be conquered with the knowing that all is well, and preparing for the great awakening.

Once we turn in the light of that great truth and face the Light of Love—throwing ourselves into its warmth and caring shelter—nothing can harm or steal the peace it can bring. It is once again down to the inner belief that *'Life Loves Me.'* Find that within or through the wonderful exercises of mirror work, meditation, and other modalities. Then, even the most terrible storms of this life will never be able to steal your knowing and inner peace.

Face the light. Let nothing turn your gaze. The miracle of the transformation of thought from fear into love is there. It is ready to manifest its eternal peace. Nothing can harm or destroy the *Loving* energy that is you!

The Tapestry of Life

'Without faith, hope and trust, there is no promise for the future, and without a promising future, life has no meaning and no justification.' —Adlin Sinclair

When everything seems like it is going wrong, when failure and discouragement is on every side, think of this story and remember: *'Life Loves You!'*

There was a young princess bursting with the joys of life and inspired to find her purpose, her quest in life. She knew that she had a grand calling to fulfil.

First was her challenge, to find the details of that calling. It was to be a special gift for her father the King. After a time of searching and pondering in her beautiful heart, seeking inside for inspiration, she knew she had it—to create a tapestry with beautiful pictures, telling a beautiful message, a story of life. This was, she felt, a holy endeavour to create a work of great beauty. She knew it could take many months for such beauty to be conveyed onto the cloth. She would need to use so many threads. Each has a purpose, each one a little part of the whole—each fulfilling its own place in the grand design and contributing to the finished masterpiece. Once envisioned, it was time to bring this picture from thought into her world.

She set about this project with great passion, gathering the many coloured threads needed and weaving the massive plain backing cloth, which was to support the entire project. Sometimes, the foundation takes the longest. Finding, creating, and preparing all these resources took time and effort and finally, she was ready to proceed.

She so wanted it to be perfect and applied every care, but her troubles soon began. As hard as she applied all her studied skills, things never seemed to come out right. Each time a thread ran out, there had to be a knot, each time a change of colour, the extra ends seemed to dangle out, making it look untidy, destroying her so perfect plans of getting it to look just right.

For a while she carried on, then slowly, the ever-increasing voices in her head were telling her it wasn't working. It would never be right—it was all a big mess. At times- her discouragement gave way to frustration, procrastination and tears of self-doubt. Other things and the necessities of life often got in the way, and the once grand project—which was to be the special present for her father—at times seemed like a millstone of discouragement, a heavy burden that once slowed down was almost impossible to push and get moving again.

Fortunately, she persevered. In spite of all her trials and discouragements, even at one point running out of the threads she needed, and the delays of having to find more. Then eventually, the project was finished. Rather than celebrating, she was very sad. The trouble was, when she looked at it, she was almost ashamed of the ragged, knotted work she had produced. She even thought of throwing the whole thing away. She was in tears, judging it and herself of no worth.

A surprise visit of her father to her workshop caught her off guard and she attempted to hide it, but it was too late. 'What is that my daughter?' he asked. She said, 'Oh it's nothing' and he grasped it, 'Let me see.' And he lifted it between them. In awe and amazement, he said, 'This is surely the most beautiful work I have ever seen.' He gazed in wonder at each thread so painstakingly applied, each in their perfect position, for he was viewing the other side of her beautiful tapestry— the finished work which she had only dreamed of. She had never seen it, except in her mind's eye, the incredible beauty of this, the perfect side of her labour of love. All her time had been spent labouring and looking at the working side of her tapestry of life—where the rough edges of life's battles and trials seemed to have marred the entire picture.

In spite of all her fears and self-doubt her creation was now finished—in its perfection and beauty. It was to hang in the Kings Feast chamber for many years, admired by and a lesson to all. If only they could all see everything that had gone into the making and the story of this beautiful work.

How often do we lose the vision of all that is being created and accomplished through our labours of love? What was the picture, you may ask. It was a mountain with sheep and a shepherd guarding, protecting and feeding his flock, on a steep, treacherous and craggy landscape. It bore the caption: 'Nothing shall hurt or destroy in all of My Holy Mountain.'

The Mystery of the Temples and Life

'I looked in temples, churches and mosques. I found the Divine within my heart.' — Rumi

This is a message I received while meditating in Khajuraho, India, a world heritage site with many beautiful, old and sacred temples.

I am *Life*. Yes, throughout all ages men have wanted to reach God, touch the divine, and feel their purpose and fulfilment.

Some have seen and understood, and yet the masses have been seduced into following and giving their divinity and power to others, called to worship in temples made by hands and give of their sustenance to leaders, many of whom were not interested in sharing these gifts with those who needed them, and many religions have been born. Stories and parables have been created as signposts for true seekers to find.

They hold many truths and also many falsehoods, created sometimes in error, when passing the message and sometimes by design, seeking power, riches and glory, rather than truth. Many beautiful buildings, though hollow edifices made of cold stone; yet often also symbols and pictures, there for the true seekers to see.

Yet you are the temple of God, or of Life. The very spark of life is entrusted to you, beating within every cell of your body. Yes, the entire universe is within you. Everything in the outer world is recorded in the universe of every cell of your being. Rejoice—you are the being of God.

Now many, sadly, have turned the meaning of that word and it has been buried under the prejudice created by false gods and false delusions of a wrathful, angry, judgemental deity whose pleasure is to punish the wicked. But can you find that truth inside your beautiful beating heart? The life-giving joy that can erupt within you after the throwing off of the shackles of guilt—that guilt was put there by those seeking to control you, to keep you in bondage and blind to the truth. God is Love, is Light, Is Life.

Feel the power of that life within. And know that the whole of you is pulsing with the vibrations of the entire cosmos that nothing can destroy, the energy of that Love itself—which continues long after the earthly vehicle and the illusion, even of a physical temple, has crumbled into the death of the ages.

Look deep inside. Connect with that Eternal Being, which is You and Life itself—and Live.

Death – The Ultimate Journey

'Life is but a blip on the radar screen of eternity . . . There is so much more . . .' – Randi G. Fine

Dedicated to Wayne Dyer, May 10, 1940–August 30, 2015. *'We are not human beings in search of a spiritual experience. We are spiritual beings immersed in a human experience.'* He is one of my favourite teachers. I received the following thoughts in the early hours, a few days before he passed.

Strangely enough, it is the fear of death that paralyses many people's enjoyment and freedom throughout life. In most cases though, the people left behind are the ones that suffer. That is when it becomes all about their loss or beliefs of loss, which of course can be very traumatic. Somehow, we have all become too focussed on the smaller picture of life here, which only includes this short stage in our ultimate journeys.

At core, we are love, which is energy. Even science teaches that 'energy cannot be destroyed, it can only change form!' So death, or better labelled 'passing'—a finishing of this earthly journey, is just the time when the core or soul energy of our being is parted from its spacecraft and returns to source.

In many cultures, this is viewed as a time for the celebration of the life of that celestial voyager, not a time of mourning, of personal loss. Isn't it almost selfish at the time of a dear soul's passing, to be thinking so much of our own losses?

It has been said that death is like sleeping and we shall all wake up. I have a feeling that it's actually us on this voyage that are more in that sleep state. Most people have forgotten the truths about the reality of our beings—but not the 'dead' who are once again in a timeless state and have already woken up.

I believe that we have been involved in the planning of every detail of our life's journey, and then chosen to forget, so that the excitement and decisions of the voyage can be unfolded like a movie. After all, movies are never the same when you already know the ending!

Many of us though, receive little glimpses in déjà-vu experiences, dreams that confirm our instructions in the night, or seeing the synchronicities that emerge along our paths.

Of course, all of these thoughts are just beliefs, but consider for a moment which serves you the best and enhances your current journey: a belief in total nothingness and obliteration, with a sudden ending—which by the way is scientifically impossible; or a belief in an awakening into the knowledge of our true beings, a graduation from life's hardships and tests? Much of this awakening in various degrees, as an aside, can happen long before physical death when installing better beliefs, actions, and energy.

There have been so many documented, amazing testimonies and stories of people's experiences when clinically dead or experiencing near death traumas, that it is becoming almost impossible to hang onto the old beliefs, that there is nothing more, after the curtain from our earthly performance closes.

Let us return to celebrating death as the passing on from this life and earthly journey. It's just like climbing out of our spacecraft at the end of a long and sometimes taxing voyage. Let us shed every fear and thus be free again and ease all the burdens of loss and despair. We can then rejoice when our dear ones have parted, with the knowledge of their and our eternal beings, dancing together again in the wonders of forever. If truth were known, we are all one, and never parted anyway!

Void, Nothingness, or a Place of Loving Energy?

'I am not my thoughts, emotions, sense perceptions and experiences; I am not the content of my life. I am Life, I am the space in which all things happen. I am consciousness. I am the Now. I Am.' – Eckhart Tolle

There are a lot of beliefs that the ultimate state, in enlightenment, is a place of void or nothingness. I have come to question this.

My belief has become that the ultimate is a place of pure Loving energy—manifesting itself, in whatever form it chooses. Everything the thinking stuff that all is made of is energy! It is considered a scientific fact that energy cannot be destroyed; it can just change its form. In effect, energy is all things, and all things are comprised of energy. It is movement and life, so how can the ultimate be a void or nothingness? Yes, this could be a great place to meditate without distraction, but even there, there has to be something, even if only the observer. Maybe a place without desire, but then surely, Loving energy has the desire to Love, to move, to be?

Again, these are my beliefs and of course we can all choose, think, and thus experience whatever we would like, so maybe the point is immaterial.

For me a life of Love, being, and experiencing all the wonders it can create and enjoy—that seems to be a great purpose and a Divine calling. I'm just curious, what kind of forever would you like to live?

You Never Lose by Giving

'At the end of the day it's not about what you have or even what you've accomplished … It's about who you've lifted up, who you've made better. It's about what you've given back.' – Denzel Washington

In most cases, this is another great belief and a standard to live by. Jesus said to 'Give to him that asks and from him that takes, to ask not again.' Most wise teachers and prophets have shared similar teaching with their followers. It also seems to be another of the things that, contrary to natural expectations, work in our universe. Would think you could find a greater wealth by giving? Surely, giving is the ultimate act of *Love*!

Now this is not just about giving money, although where possible it can be a good start—without it many noble projects and organisations couldn't survive. More important though is giving our love, attention, and time. It seems the whole of life is keen to teach us these lessons. We start life as selfish babies, where our entire survival is dependent on others and then, if our needs are not met, we scream or cry until they are. Sadly, many children never learn the lessons of sharing, which often come along in a big way when a first sibling, and also if others arrive.

Later in life, relationship could be the next great lesson in sharing. Many people have said that the only way to be successful in relationships is not just to give 50 per cent or even 90 or 95 per cent, but to be prepared to give 100 per cent! If we all had this attitude, then we could be pretty sure of success in our relationships. With both the giving and receiving of gratitude and love, many more relationships would have the chance to grow and prosper.

The next test or lesson of *love* and sacrifice comes with bearing children and the huge amount of love and many sacrifices needed to successfully rear and care for other lives. The love of a mother is often pictured as an ultimate form of love. It is giving one's life for another; in this case every day, rather than our ultimate picture of heroism, giving one's life for another in a sudden act of bravery.

Now there is a balance in this, as some have given so much there may be nothing, or almost nothing left to give. Self love is such an important lesson also, giving to oneself, taking time to recharge and being filled with Love in that special place within. Otherwise, there may soon only be an empty shell left.

It is important to give out of love, for giving out of duty, or by being too full of the idea of personal gain, or from a place of resentment or bitterness, instead of true love surely has no reward. Like with everything, when we move away from Love, there is only cold darkness left. Sadly, it seems our modern world has become a very selfish place. The values of Love and giving are frequently lost in the quick fix of personal gain and instant gratification.

There is a beautiful lesson filled movie called 'The Fourth Wise Man.' It is about the wise men who went on a pilgrimage to give the baby Jesus gifts, and especially the story of one who didn't make it to present his gift. All along he was faced with the choice of the sacrifice of his calling and purpose, which he thought was to give his gift to Jesus—or the choice to help others. As it turned out, in every time of choice, he gave his gifts to others, he spent his life making many sacrifices. Eventually, when close to death, he was feeling he had failed and was dying in poverty. As he finally met Jesus, he ashamedly shared his sorrow of failure, but was shown that all he had done, throughout his life for others, was truly all given to his Lord. His reward was coming, and in many cases already there, in seeing the fruits of his love.

Oh that we could also *Love* in such ways. There is a beautiful little song 'Except a corn of wheat fall in the ground and die, it abideth alone, but if it die, it bringeth forth much fruit.' Through Love we can experience much of the true meaning of *life*!

All You Need Is Love

'The Greatest of these is Love.' – The Bible

The Beatles sang it, or just repeated it. So many wise men, prophets, scholars, authors, poets, scientists, and just ordinary people, have echoed it. This simple, yet profound message, comes, broadcasting in, throughout time, from the annals of history and reaches us today.

I believe it to be the most quintessential truth one can discover. Why else would we journey through this planet and solar system? Nature cries it! We circle a hot sun; a ball of almost unlimited energy, without it life would cease to exist. Its very essence and energy is the magical component of the growth of every plant and again, the building block of all life. Our earth's position is ideal. We orbit perfectly in a place between a cold frozen wasteland, and a fiery hell. This too, is a picture of Love. If we stray too far, to either side, we can burn up in the fires of jealousy or have our heart wither in a cold, lonely, frozen desert.

We can't see love, or can we? We can feel its warmth in a smile and see its effects and the changes created by its energy. It can warm a life and melt the hardest heart. Yet often we isolate ourselves against it in fear of being hurt or being consumed by all the changes it can bring.

Healing modalities use its power. They are sending the power and vibration of love from one heart and being to another. Sending it, through time and space, to touch another beings stuck energy and resonate together, so both can once more vibrate in unison with the very nature of things, which is Love.

Religious texts teach us that if what we do is without love, we are nothing. I believe God, Spirit, Energy and any other label you would like to give the Divine, is *Love*. In fact, as scientists have proved that everything is energy, it is then

148

easy to interpolate that all things are energy. We are part of those All Things. This is the magical place where science and most spiritual teachers meet. We are a part of God! Our root being and our core is *Love*. Maybe we have to journey there, through many dark ages of our own creation, seeking so many other ways to come back to this fundamental truth.

As we seek to live it, through personal growth or spirituality, I believe we can reconnect with the entirety of ourselves. Realising the Kingdom of Heaven, or Bliss, or Nirvana, is within. Again, substitute this with whatever label or word picture you prefer. All the projections or the hologram of our thoughts without are just a playground, a world experience, giving us choices and many learnings on our route back to discovering, realisation, and the owning of what we have been, and in essence, are all along.

I believe the only law in creation is to Love, as some would say; 'God's only Law is Love!'

How we play out these earthly roles now and in the illusions of pasts and futures are of no significant consequence to the greatest truth that we are, and I am, the loving energy that comprises all things!

Where Are You Choosing to Live?

'Heaven on earth is a choice you must make, not a place you must find!' – Wayne Dyer

There is an interesting saying, 'Heaven is where your heart is.' There appears to be two quite different places we can live, or maybe I can say the belief systems we can inhabit. There is also a crossover period, times when we are living in either dimension, or in places between the two.

There is the earthly realm—we all inhabit here—before what can be a kind of an awakening. This is when all our beliefs and feelings are centred on life in that earthly realm—mainly without an awareness of our deeper existence as spiritual beings. Here we are completely identifying with the human experience. All our beliefs and experiences are centred on living as a human and the earthly journey. This time is usually and mainly lived in ego and accompanied by the fear of death, illness, and subject to many of life's more basic needs and passions; food, shelter, power and earthly riches. These, by the way, also tend to come with many earthly problems, troubles, and fears of loss. It is a world where certainty is elusive and nothing appears permanent, which it isn't!

Then, there can be a period of awakening or realisation of different core beliefs, values, and realm of being. This is where we are becoming aware of our true nature—that heavenly being, in our earthly spaceship on a journey of experience, growth, and pleasure in this temporal illusionary earthly domain.

When we are truly awake and heaven-centred, our belief system holds no more fear! After all, what can harm an eternal being, a part of the eternal life force, or energy of Love—which could, if you like, be called God?

Sometimes, this takes a physical death. However, as many of us are changing and awakening faster now, I believe we can live far more—even whilst still here on earth—in that heavenly realm. From this perspective of heaven within, and with all the associated beliefs, we have already crossed over. We have discovered that heaven is where our heart is, inside of our beings—likewise, it can also be experienced from inside the spacecraft, which we are now journeying in. This is living from the viewpoint of being that spirit on a human journey, rather than a human searching for a spiritual experience. From this perspective, there can be no more fear of death—which is just leaving our earthly spacecraft behind.

The miracle and awakening is the complete change of realm, or the perception of our home, or centre and core beliefs. We may not know everything about that realm or dimension and really don't need to! Our centre and being is grounded in that knowledge. We are travelling through time and space and even lifetimes, firm in the knowledge of our place in the eternal now. We have shifted from many of the thoughts, fears, values and quests of this temporary world, and have an inner knowing of the amazing powerful beings we truly are. We may have chosen to forget most of this knowing, and especially put down and temporarily left behind many of our heavenly powers, but even these are being awakened again and renewed inside us.

Thoughts create things! As we become more heaven-centred, the creation or manifestation process is speeding up. It is just as well that it is not so quickly manifested in our previous earthly centred state, as often felt fears and other base emotions, anger and hate are already creating too many seemingly terrible experiences in the earthly realms. Fortunately, this is all a part of the illusionary playground, which like the hollow suite in Sci-Fi movies, can be changed or modified and even eventually switched off by those now more evolved thoughts.

Could it be just about where we want to dwell, or what kind of world we would like to live in? For me, it seems to be what some may call a no-brainer. I will choose a life centred around a belief system or heavenly dimension of the Eternal—a Love-filled realm where all things work together for good, and all desires are met. The core of this is a place where I love myself and I know—Life itself Loves me. When that shift is complete, I can dip in and out of life's wonderful experiences, enjoying all its pleasures and sensory thrills, confident in the powerful knowledge that I am living in Love. Then I know that nothing can hurt or destroy in that Holy Mountain. I am living life in a far more real realm, in the knowledge of the powerful spirit that I am, and we are.

I may even choose to forget for a while, on another run through life, knowing at any time I am in, or can, and will come back to that beautiful heaven which is filled with wonders, the place of source being. Let's join together there again in that heavenly dimension, where, if truth were fully remembered, we have never even left.

It's Time for the 'What If Game.' – Review Questions

Here are the last review questions. Would it be okay to take the time to listen for answers and leadings on these questions? The answers you receive may well give you inspired plans and directions to follow.

What if I could focus more on the now, rather than striving for the future?

What if I could do, be, or have anything, what would I ask for?

What if I created a vision board? What are the pictures, visions and desires I would like to incorporate?

What if I lived my vision with passion and persistence? What could then be accomplished?

What if I no longer worried about people's opinions of me?

What if I found that place of perfect peace? How smooth would life's journey be?

What if I could see the bigger picture, a view from the Spirit of my life? What peace and joy would that bring?

What if everything can be discovered, with the realisation that I am the Temple of God?

What if death was a cause for a celebration of the life of those departed, and there was always knowledge of our lasting connections?

What if I could choose, what kind of forever would I like to live?

What if I never lose by giving? What is the gift to others and the world that I can give?

What if Love is the greatest thing? How can I be more loving?

What if I could choose, which realm would I live in most of the time?

IN CONCLUSION

Thank you for sharing in this journey of exploration and growth. I know its ideas have been wonderful milestones in my own journey, and trust that some of them will have spoken to you. Please let me know what you liked best and what they are changing in your life. I'd love to hear too, your favourite 'What If' questions and their answers.

Review this book from time to time, it's amazing how the things that speak to us change as we evolve and grow. Lend it, or recommend it to friends, or anyone you meet who may benefit from the growth, solutions, and wisdom shared.

Be sure to keep loving, learning, growing and giving, as these are the main purpose of Life.

I wish you all the very best in your growth, journey, and awakening. This is just the beginning!

~Keith Higgs

Please visit our Facebook community, which is for anyone who has read the book. You will find us at www.Facebook. com/groups/FlyBacktoLove. You will need to ask to join, as it is a private group, so that the lessons shared can be more personal. Share you thoughts, insights and growth there, that all may benefit. There will also be posted notification of events, book signings and workshops.

Soon to be available—I'm recording an audio copy of the book. Watch out for news of this.

I'm also the administrator of a public Facebook group 'Awake Your Dreams.' You may like to join us there. It is full of inspiring pictures and quotes, posted by many members. It would be great to see your favourite quotes and meet you there.

Resources and Links. – Use them to stay in touch.

The book's Facebook page:
www.Facebook.com/TakeControlofYourSpacecraft

Please add a like if you haven't already.

The books Facebook community:
www.Facebook.com/groups/FlyBacktoLove

www.Facebook.com/groups/AwakeYourDreams -- For inspiring Pictures, Quotes and discussions.

The book and my blog site: www.KeithHiggs.com

Please stay in touch by signing up to our mailing list.

There will be a growing list of 'What If' questions, other news and extras, and also a few other topics posted that didn't fit in this book.

Follow us on Twitter @FlyBacktoLove

I am available for talks, workshops and private sessions.

Contact me at Keith@FlyBacktoLove.com

APPENDIX

#KeyWords
Here you will find a list of each of the topics/posts along with the #KeyWords from each of these topics/posts. These #KeyWords give more of a flavour of what each post is primarily about rather than the full list of the words included that you can find in the index.

The second list is of each #KeyWord with each topic/post it highlights. This can give a useful reading plan for the subjects listed.

Section 1. Understanding Your Spacecraft   1
Driving Your Vehicle—What Is in Control?   2
#Control #Decisions #Programming #Choice #Autopilot #Consciousness

Your Spacecraft   4
#Decisions #Autopilot #Beliefs #Fears #Voices

How Much Are You Worth?   5
#Value #Self Worth #Voices #Habits

We Are Running on Autopilot   7
#Autopilot #Fears #Subconscious Mind #Control

The Voices in our Heads   10
#Thoughts #Choice #Direction #Observer #Beliefs #Dreams #Love #Fear

Who Is the Pilot Today?   11
#Archetypes #Inner Child #Observer #Personalities #Control

The Fear of Change   12
#Fear #Change #Comfort Zones #Conformity #Destiny #Success
#Decision

**Are Your Gauges of Wealth, Happiness and Success
Stuck?**   13
#Wealth #Success #Happiness #Conformity #Limiting Beliefs
#Unworthiness

**Have You Ever Wondered Why You Don't Seem to be in
Control?**   15
#Control #Centre #Balance #Ego #Personalities #Purpose #Desire

Are You Making Your Own Decisions?   17
#Control #Decisions #Programming #Choice

Do You Believe, That You Can Fly?   18
#Fear #Change #Self Confidence #Success #Beliefs #Faith
#Failure

Section 2. Some Guidelines for Flight and Maintenance   22
Honour the Crew in Your Spacecraft   23
#Ego #Roles #Commander #Love #Honour #Appreciation

We Are Meaning Making Machines   24
#Meaning #Reason #Blame #Thoughts #Beliefs

First Steps in Reprogramming Your Autopilot   26
#Mindfulness #Choices #Decisions #Thoughts #Affirmations

Be Aware! Your Fears Can Create Your Next Reality   28
#Fears #Reality #Letting Go #Imagination #Manifestation

Letting Go   30
#Blocks #Fear #Healing #Release #Change

Love or Fear, Your Choice   31
#Love #Fear #Light #Darkness #Choice #Friends

What Is Disease?   33
#Disease #Thoughts #Feelings #Energy #Affirmations #Gratitude #Habits

Stuck Energy Can Move Again!   36
#Energy #Healing #Beliefs #Attitude #Disease #Medicine

Stop Beating Yourself Up!   38
#Happiness #Remorse #Thinking #Indecision

Failure, or Another Disguised Step Forward?   39
#Failure #Success #Happiness #Disappointment #Growth #Change

No Is Almost Never Personal!   41
#Rejection #Humiliation #Fears #No #Love #Compassion #

What Are You Looking For and What Do You Notice?   44
#Injustice #Anxiety #Stress #Focus #Complaint #Thoughts

Improve It! Don't Attempt to Fix It!   45
#Focus #Circumstances #Fix it #Improve #Habits #Gratitude

Working Your Way to Heaven Won't Work!   47
#Religion #Works #Heaven #Laughter #Love #Forgiveness #Rituals

Shit Happens!   49
#Learning #Stuck #Lessons #Choice #Experiences

Hold On! The Crown, the Fruit, and the Rewards Are On Their Way!   50
#Persistence #Faith #Rewards #Success #Determination #Victory #Results #Growth

Section 3. Taking Control 55
Take Responsibility! 56
#Responsibility #Blame #Success #Happiness #Beliefs #Empowerment #Direction

Ask How 57
#How #Question #Desire #Faith #Expectation

What Does It Take to Become Free? 59
#Limiting Beliefs #Beliefs #Choice #Habits #Voices

Two Things That Will Crash Your Spacecraft 61
#Judgement #Bitterness #Self Righteousness #Forgiveness #Beliefs

Two Enemies of a Smooth Ride, in the Right Now 63
#Past #Future #Focus #Memories #Thoughts #Now

What do You Fill and Programme Your World With? 66
#Detox #Cleansing #News #Association

Be Careful What You Focus On! 68
#Thoughts #Intentions #Focus #Affirmations #Change #Fears

Sincere Heart Cry, Can Change Your World 71
#Heart Cry #Change #Answer #Hope #Tears #Surrender #Fears #Darkness #Prayer

Change Is Just One Heartbeat Away . . . But? 74
#Change #Commitment #Desire #Beliefs #Comfort

There Is an Ancient Practice That Can Change Your World 77
#Ho'oponopono #Forgiveness #Love #Change #Responsibility #Cleansing

No More Trying—Just Do It! 79
#Try #Believe #Will #Success #Failure #Commitment

Why Shouldn't We? 81
#Should #Have To #Need #Conscience #Judgement

The Power of Prayer 82
#Prayer #Intention #Energy #Power #God

Choose Empowering Beliefs 84
#Beliefs #Choice #Thoughts #Feelings #Responsible

It's Time to Take Action! But How? 86
#Action #Empowerment #Love #Life

Take Action Anyway! 87
#Action #Indecision #Consequences #Failure #Choices

What Holds Us in the Darkness? 88
#Darkness #Light #Love #Fear #Rebirth #Healing #Belief

What Needs to be Shed to Bring Us into the Light? 89
#Light #Illusion #Love #Fear #Awakening #Beliefs

Section 4. Flying in Style 92
The Law of Attraction 93
#Law Of Attraction #Dreams #Desires #Thoughts #Habits #The
Secret #Mindfulness

Empowerment 95
#Helpers #Anointing #Angels #Guides

What Will You Wear Today? 96
#Emotions #Habits #Choices #Happiness

The Mystery of Money 97
#Money #Understanding #Wealth #Value #Energy

Have You Found Your Golden Goose? 99
#Financial Freedom #Abundance #Wealth #MLM #Network
Marketing #Time Freedom

The Pursuit of Happiness 103
#Happiness #Wealth #Wisdom #Life #Religion

Sex, Nudity, Freedom, and the Divine   105
#Sex #Nudity #Freedom #Divine #Programming #Beliefs #Choices
#Control

Forgiveness Is Loving Ourselves!   107
#Forgiveness #Healing #Love #Self Love #Cleansing #Bitterness

Are You Planning Your Life?   109
#Vision #Purpose #Goals #Life #Success #Desires #Ideals
#Dreams

**Past Lives or Seeing Through the Eyes of Others that Have
Been Before?**   111
#Reincarnation #Spirit Guide #Past Lives #Mysteries #Experiences

Do You Desire a Soul Mate?   112
#Soulmate #Desire #Love #Beliefs #Lonely #Passion #Oneness
#Relationship

**Some Tips and Ideas Experienced from My Soul Mate
Manifestation Process**   114
#Soulmate #Dating # Love # Lonely #Age #Beliefs #Relationship

Integrity—Live in Truth   116
#Integrity #Truth #Thought #Direction #Lying

I Am   118
#Affirmations #Beliefs #God #Values #Self Talk #Law of Attraction

For Those Suffering Loss   120
#Loss #Death #Suffering #New Beginnings #Beliefs #Bereavement
#Grief

Section 5. Fly Back to Love   124
**Reaching Your Idea of Heaven Is Not the Goal—It's Enjoying
the Journey!**   125
#Goals #Success #Heaven #Achievement #Enjoyment

An Adventure in Goal Setting   127
#Vision #Purpose #Goals # Manifestation #Success #Comfort
Zone #Mediocrity

Have You Created a Vision Board?   130
#Vision Board #Manifestation #Goals #Desires #Dreams

How Do You See the World?   132
#Mediocrity #Routine #Vision #Dreams

The Ramblings of a Mad Man   134
#Genius #Insanity #Conformity #Madness

Perfect Peace in the Midst of a Storm   135
#Peace #Life #Storms #Trust #Love #Fear #Faith

The Tapestry of Life   137
#Beliefs #Trust #Perseverance #Gratitude #Life #Faith
#Confidence

The Mystery of the Temples and Life   140
#Temples #Life #God #Love #Religion # Purpose

Death – The Ultimate Journey   142
#Death #Eternity #Eternal Life #Loss #Grief #Mourning
#Bereavement

Void, Nothingness, or a Place of Loving Energy?   144
#Enlightenment #Heaven #Void #Nothingness #Love #Forever

You Never Lose by Giving   145
#Giving #Give #Love #Sacrifice #Relationship #Gratification
#Selfishness

All You Need Is Love   148
#Love #Heaven #Energy #Spirit #God

Where Are You Choosing to Live?   150
#Heaven #Awakening #Choice #Heart #Eternity #Spirit #Love

#KeyWords from the Posts/Topics

Note: This list is more of a guide of what each topic/post is about. See the following index for places where the words are used in the full text.

#Abundance
Have You Found Your Golden Goose?   99

#Achievement
Reaching Your Idea of Heaven Is Not the Goal—It's Enjoying the Journey!   125

#Action
It's Time to Take Action! But How?   86
Take Action Anyway!   87

#Affirmations
Be Careful What You Focus On!   68
First Steps in Reprogramming Your Autopilot   26
I Am   118
What Is Disease?   33

#Age
Some Tips and Ideas Experienced from My Soul Mate Manifestation Process   114

#Angels
Empowerment   95

#Anointing
Empowerment   95

#Answer
Sincere Heart Cry, Can Change Your World   71

#Anxiety
What Are You Looking For and What Do You Notice?   44

#Appreciation
Honour the Crew in Your Spacecraft   23

#Archetypes
Who Is the Pilot Today?   11

#Association
What do You Fill and Program Your World With?   62

#Attitude
Stuck Energy Can Move Again!   36

#Autopilot
Driving Your Vehicle—What Is in Control?   2
We Are Running on Autopilot   7
Your Spacecraft   4

#Awakening
What Needs to be Shed to Bring Us into the Light?   89
Where Are You Choosing to Live?   150

#Balance
Have You Ever Wondered Why You Don't Seem to be in Control?   15

#Beliefs
Change Is Just One Heartbeat Away . . . But?   74
Choose Empowering Beliefs   84
Do You Believe That You Can Fly?   18
Do You Desire a Soul Mate?   112
For Those Suffering Loss   120
I Am   118
Sex, Nudity, Freedom, and the Divine   105
Some Tips and Ideas Experienced from My Soul Mate Manifestation Process   114
Stuck Energy Can Move Again!   36
Take Responsibility!   56
The Tapestry of Life   137
The Voices in our Heads   10
Two Things That Will Crash Your Spacecraft   61
We Are Meaning Making Machines   24
What Does It Take to Become Free?   59
What Holds Us in the Darkness?   88

What Needs to be Shed to Bring Us into the Light?   89
Your Spacecraft   4

#Believe
No More Trying—Just Do It!   79

#Bereavement
For Those Suffering Loss   120
Death – The Ultimate Journey   142

#Bitterness
Two Things That Will Crash Your Spacecraft   61
Forgiveness Is Loving Ourselves!   107

#Blame
Take Responsibility!   56
We Are Meaning Making Machines   24

#Blocks
Letting Go   30

#Centre
Have You Ever Wondered Why You Don't Seem to be in Control?   15

#Change
Be Careful What You Focus On!   68
Change Is Just One Heartbeat Away . . . But?   74
Do You Believe That You Can Fly?   18
Failure, or Another Disguised Step Forward?   39
Letting Go   30
Sincere Heart Cry, Can Change Your World   71
The Fear of Change   12
There Is an Ancient Practice that Can Change Your World   77

#Choice
Are You Making Your Own Decisions?   17
Choose Empowering Beliefs   84
Driving Your Vehicle—What Is in Control?   2
Love or Fear, Your Choice   31

Shit Happens!   49
The Voices in our Heads   10
What Does It Take to Become Free?   59
Where Are You Choosing to Live?   150
First Steps in Reprogramming Your Autopilot   26
Sex, Nudity, Freedom, and the Divine   105
Take Action Anyway!   87
What Will You Wear Today?   96

#Circumstances
Improve It! Don't Attempt to Fix It!   45

#Cleansing
Forgiveness Is Loving Ourselves!   107
There Is an Ancient Practice that Can Change Your World   77
What do You Fill and Program Your World With?   62

#Comfort
Change Is Just One Heartbeat Away . . . But?   74

#Comfort Zone
An Adventure in Goal Setting   127
The Fear of Change   12

#Commander
Honour the Crew in Your Spacecraft   23

#Commitment
Change Is Just One Heartbeat Away . . . But?   74

#Commitment
No More Trying—Just Do It!   79
No Is Almost Never Personal!   41

#Complaint
What Are You Looking For and What Do You Notice?   44

#Confidence
The Tapestry of Life   137

#Conformity
Are Your Gauges of Wealth, Happiness and Success Stuck?   13
The Fear of Change   12
The Ramblings of a Mad Man   134

#Conscience
Why Shouldn't We?   81

#Consciousness
Driving Your Vehicle—What Is in Control?   2

#Consequences
Take Action Anyway!   87

#Control
Are You Making Your Own Decisions?   17
Driving Your Vehicle—What Is in Control?   2
Have You Ever Wondered Why You Don't Seem to be in Control?   15
Sex, Nudity, Freedom, and the Divine   105
We Are Running on Autopilot   7
Who Is the Pilot Today?   11

#Darkness
Sincere Heart Cry, Can Change Your World   71
Love or Fear, Your Choice   31
What Holds Us in the Darkness?   88

#Dating
Some Tips and Ideas Experienced from My Soul Mate Manifestation Process   114

#Death
Death – The Ultimate Journey   142
For Those Suffering Loss   120

#Decisions
The Fear of Change   12
Are You Making Your Own Decisions?   17
Driving Your Vehicle—What Is in Control?   2
First Steps in Reprogramming Your Autopilot   26

Your Spacecraft   4

#Desires
Ask How   57
Change Is Just One Heartbeat Away . . . But?   74
Do You Desire a Soul Mate?   112
Have You Ever Wondered Why You Don't Seem to be in Control?   15
Are You Planning Your Life?   109
Have You Created a Vision Board?   130
The Law of Attraction   93

#Destiny
The Fear of Change   12

#Determination
Hold On! The Crown, the Fruit, and the Rewards Are On Their Way!   50

#Detox
What do You Fill and Program Your World With?   62

#Direction
Integrity—Live in Truth   116
Take Responsibility!   56
The Voices in our Heads   10

#Disappointment
Failure, or Another Disguised Step Forward?   39

#Disease
Stuck Energy Can Move Again!   36
What Is Disease?   33

#Divine
Sex, Nudity, Freedom, and the Divine   105

#Dreams
Are You Planning Your Life?   109

Have You Created a Vision Board?   130
How Do You See the World?   132
The Law of Attraction   93
The Voices in our Heads   10

#Ego
Have You Ever Wondered Why You Don't Seem to be in Control?   15
Honour the Crew in Your Spacecraft   23

#Emotions
What Will You Wear Today?   96

#Empowerment
It's Time to Take Action! But How?   86
Take Responsibility!   56

#Energy
All You Need Is Love   148
Stuck Energy Can Move Again!   36
The Mystery of Money   97
The Power of Prayer   82
What Is Disease?   33

#Enjoyment
Reaching Your Idea of Heaven Is Not the Goal—It's Enjoying the Journey!   125

#Enlightenment
Void, Nothingness, or a Place of Loving Energy?   144

#Eternal Life
Death – The Ultimate Journey   142

#Eternity
Death – The Ultimate Journey   142
Where Are You Choosing to Live?   150

#Expectation
Ask How   57

#Experiences
Past Lives or Seeing Through the Eyes of Others that Have Been Before?   111
Shit Happens!   49

#Failure
Do You Believe, That You Can Fly?   18
Failure, or Another Disguised Step Forward?   39
No More Trying—Just Do It!   79
Take Action Anyway!   87

#Faith
Ask How   57
Do You Believe, That You Can Fly?   18
Hold On! The Crown, the Fruit, and the Rewards Are On Their Way!   50
Perfect Peace in the Midst of a Storm   135
The Tapestry of Life   137

#Fear
Do You Believe, That You Can Fly?   18
Letting Go   30
Love or Fear, Your Choice   31
Perfect Peace in the Midst of a Storm   135
The Fear of Change   12
The Voices in our Heads   10
What Holds Us in the Darkness?   88
What Needs to be Shed to Bring Us into the Light?   89
Be Aware! Your Fears Can Create Your Next Reality   28
Be Careful What You Focus On!   68
No Is Almost Never Personal!   41
Sincere Heart Cry, Can Change Your World   71
We Are Running on Autopilot   7
Your Spacecraft   4

#Feelings
Choose Empowering Beliefs   84
What Is Disease?   33

#Financial Freedom
Have You Found Your Golden Goose?   99

#Fix it
Improve It! Don't Attempt to Fix It!   45

#Focus
Be Careful What You Focus On!   68
Improve It! Don't Attempt to Fix It!   45
Two Enemies of a Smooth Ride, in the Right Now   63
What Are You Looking For and What Do You Notice?   44

#Forever
Void, Nothingness, or a Place of Loving Energy?   144

#Forgiveness
Forgiveness Is Loving Ourselves!   107
There Is an Ancient Practice that Can Change Your World   77
Two Things That Will Crash Your Spacecraft   61
Working Your Way to Heaven Won't Work!   47

#Freedom
Sex, Nudity, Freedom, and the Divine   105

#Friends
Love or Fear, Your Choice   31

#Future
Two Enemies of a Smooth Ride, in the Right Now   63

#Genius
The Ramblings of a Mad Man   134

#Giving
You Never Lose by Giving   145

#Goals
An Adventure in Goal Setting   127
Are You Planning Your Life?   109
Have You Created a Vision Board?   130
Reaching Your Idea of Heaven Is Not the Goal—It's Enjoying the Journey!   125

#God
All You Need Is Love   148
I Am   118
The Mystery of the Temples and Life   140
The Power of Prayer   82

#Gratitude
You Never Lose by Giving   145
Improve It! Don't Attempt to Fix It!   45
The Tapestry of Life   137
What Is Disease?   33

#Grief
Death – The Ultimate Journey   142
For Those Suffering Loss   120

#Growth
Failure, or Another Disguised Step Forward?   39
Hold On! The Crown, the Fruit, and the Rewards Are On Their Way!   50

#Guides
Empowerment   95

#Habits
How Much Are You Worth?   5
Improve It! Don't Attempt to Fix It!   45
The Law of Attraction   93
What Does It Take to Become Free?   59
What Is Disease?   33
What Will You Wear Today?   96

#Happiness
Are Your Gauges of Wealth, Happiness & Success Stuck?   13
Failure, or Another Disguised Step Forward?   39
Stop Beating Yourself Up!   38
Take Responsibility!   56
The Pursuit of Happiness   103
What Will You Wear Today?   96

#Have To
Why Shouldn't We?   81
Forgiveness Is Loving Ourselves!   107
Letting Go   30
Stuck Energy Can Move Again!   36
What Holds Us in the Darkness?   88

#Heart Cry
Sincere Heart Cry, Can Change Your World   71

#Heart
Where Are You Choosing to Live?   150

#Heaven
All You Need Is Love   148
Reaching Your Idea of Heaven Is Not the Goal—It's Enjoying the Journey!   125
Void, Nothingness, or a Place of Loving Energy?   144
Where Are You Choosing to Live?   150
Working Your Way to Heaven Won't Work!   47

#Helpers
Empowerment   95

#Ho'oponopono
There Is an Ancient Practice that Can Change Your World   77

#Honour
Honour the Crew in Your Spacecraft   23

#Hope
Sincere Heart Cry, Can Change Your World   71

#How
Ask How   57

#Humiliation
No Is Almost Never Personal!   41

#Ideals
Are You Planning Your Life?   109

#Illusion
What Needs to be Shed to Bring Us into the Light?   89

#Imagination
Be Aware! Your Fears Can Create Your Next Reality   28

#Improve
Improve It! Don't Attempt to Fix It!   45

#Indecision
Stop Beating Yourself Up!   38

Take Action Anyway!   87

#Injustice
What Are You Looking For and What Do You Notice?   44

#Inner Child
Who Is the Pilot Today?   11

#Insanity
The Ramblings of a Mad Man   134

#Integrity
Integrity—Live in Truth   116

#Intention
The Power of Prayer   82
Be Careful What You Focus On!   68

#Judgement
Two Things That Will Crash Your Spacecraft   61
Why Shouldn't We?   81

#Laughter
Working Your Way to Heaven Won't Work!   47

#Law Of Attraction
The Law of Attraction   93
I Am   118

#Learning
Shit Happens!   49

#Letting Go
Be Aware! Your Fears Can Create Your Next Reality   28

#Life
Are You Planning Your Life?   109

#Life
It's Time to Take Action! But How?   86
Perfect Peace in the Midst of a Storm   135
The Mystery of the Temples and Life   140
The Pursuit of Happiness   103
The Tapestry of Life   137

#Light
Love or Fear, Your Choice   31
What Holds Us in the Darkness?   88
What Needs to be Shed to Bring Us into the Light?   89

#Limiting Beliefs
Are Your Gauges of Wealth, Happiness and Success Stuck?   13
What Does It Take to Become Free?   59

#Lonely
Do You Desire a Soul Mate?   112
Some Tips and Ideas Experienced from My Soul Mate Manifestation Process   114

#Loss
Death – The Ultimate Journey   142
For Those Suffering Loss   120

#Love
All You Need Is Love   148
Do You Desire a Soul Mate?   112
Forgiveness Is Loving Ourselves!   107
Honour the Crew in Your Spacecraft   23
It's Time to Take Action! But How?   86
Love or Fear, Your Choice   31

No Is Almost Never Personal!   41
Perfect Peace in the Midst of a Storm   135
Some Tips and Ideas Experienced from My Soul Mate Manifestation Process   114
The Mystery of the Temples and Life   140
The Voices in our Heads   10
There Is an Ancient Practice that Can Change Your World   77
Void, Nothingness, or a Place of Loving Energy?   144
What Holds Us in the Darkness?   88
What Needs to be Shed to Bring Us into the Light?   89
Where Are You Choosing to Live?   150
Working Your Way to Heaven Won't Work!   47
You Never Lose by Giving   145

#Lying
Integrity—Live in Truth   116

#Madness
The Ramblings of a Mad Man   134

#Manifestation
An Adventure in Goal Setting   127
Be Aware! Your Fears Can Create Your Next Reality   28
Have You Created a Vision Board?   130

#Meaning
We Are Meaning Making Machines   24

#Medicine
Stuck Energy Can Move Again!   36

#Mediocrity
An Adventure in Goal Setting   127
How Do You See the World?   132

#Memories
Two Enemies of a Smooth Ride, in the Right Now   63

#Mindfulness
First Steps in Reprogramming Your Autopilot   26
The Law of Attraction   93

#MLM
Have You Found Your Golden Goose?   99

#Money
The Mystery of Money   97

#Mourning
Death – The Ultimate Journey   142

#Mysteries
Past Lives or Seeing Through the Eyes of Others that Have Been Before?   111

#Need
Why Shouldn't We?   81

#Network Marketing
Have You Found Your Golden Goose?   99

#New Beginnings
For Those Suffering Loss   120

#News
What do You Fill and Program Your World With?   62

#No
No Is Almost Never Personal!   41

#Nothingness

Void, Nothingness, or a Place of Loving Energy?   144

#Now
Two Enemies of a Smooth Ride, in the Right Now   63

#Nudity
Sex, Nudity, Freedom, and the Divine   105

#Observer
The Voices in our Heads   10
Who Is the Pilot Today?   11

#Oneness
Do You Desire a Soul Mate?   112

#Passion
Do You Desire a Soul Mate?   112

#Past Lives
Past Lives or Seeing Through the Eyes of Others that Have Been Before?   111

#Past
Two Enemies of a Smooth Ride, in the Right Now   63

#Peace
Perfect Peace in the Midst of a Storm   135

#Perseverance
The Tapestry of Life   137

#Persistence
Hold On! The Crown, the Fruit and the Rewards Are On Their Way!   37

#Personalities Who Is the Pilot Today?
Have You Ever Wondered Why You Don't Seem to be in Control?   15

#Power
The Power of Prayer   82

#Prayer
The Power of Prayer   82
Sincere Heart Cry, Can Change Your World   71

#Programming
Are You Making Your Own Decisions?   17
Driving Your Vehicle—What Is in Control?   2
Sex, Nudity, Freedom, and the Divine   105

#Purpose
An Adventure in Goal Setting   127

Are You Planning Your Life?   109
Have You Ever Wondered Why You Don't Seem to be in Control?   15
The Mystery of the Temples and Life   140

#Question
Ask How   57

#Reality
Be Aware! Your Fears Can Create Your Next Reality   28

#Reason
We Are Meaning Making Machines   24

#Rebirth
What Holds Us in the Darkness?   88

#Reincarnation
Past Lives or Seeing Through the Eyes of Others that Have Been Before?   111

#Rejection
No Is Almost Never Personal!   41

#Relationship
Do You Desire a Soul Mate?   112
Some Tips and Ideas Experienced from My Soul Mate Manifestation Process   114
You Never Lose by Giving   145

#Release
Letting Go   30

#Religion
The Mystery of the Temples and Life   140
The Pursuit of Happiness   103
Working Your Way to Heaven Won't Work!   47

#Remorse
Stop Beating Yourself Up!   38

#Responsibility
Take Responsibility!   56
There Is an Ancient Practice that Can Change Your World   77
Choose Empowering Beliefs   84

#Results
Hold On! The Crown, the Fruit and the Rewards Are On Their Way!   37

#Rewards
Hold On! The Crown, the Fruit and the Rewards Are On Their Way!   37

#Rituals
Working Your Way to Heaven Won't Work!   47

#Roles
Honour the Crew in Your Spacecraft   23

#Routine
How Do You See the World?   132

#Sacrifice
You Never Lose by Giving   145

#Self Confidence
Do You Believe That You Can Fly?   18

#Self Love
Forgiveness Is Loving Ourselves!   107

#Self Righteousness
Two Things That Will Crash Your Spacecraft   61

#Self Talk
I Am   118

#Self Worth
How Much Are You Worth?   5

#Selfishness
You Never Lose by Giving   145

#Sex
Sex, Nudity, Freedom, and the Divine   105

#Should
Why Shouldn't We?   81

#Soulmate
Do You Desire a Soul Mate?   112
Some Tips and Ideas Experienced from My Soul Mate Manifestation Process   114

#Spirit
All You Need Is Love   148

Where Are You Choosing to Live?   150

#Spirit Guide
Past Lives or Seeing Through the Eyes of Others that Have Been Before?   111

#Storms
Perfect Peace in the Midst of a Storm   135

#Stress
What Are You Looking For and What Do You Notice?   44

#Stuck
Shit Happens!   49

#Subconscious Mind
We Are Running on Autopilot   7

#Success
An Adventure in Goal Setting   127
Are You Planning Your Life?   109
Are Your Gauges of Wealth, Happiness & Success Stuck?   13
Do You Believe, That You Can Fly?   18
Failure or Another Disguised Step Forward?   39

Hold On! The Crown, the Fruit, and the Rewards Are On Their Way!   50
No More Trying—Just Do It!   79
Reaching Your Idea of Heaven Is Not the Goal—It's Enjoying the Journey!   125
Take Responsibility!   56
The Fear of Change   12

#Suffering
For Those Suffering Loss   120

#Surrender
Sincere Heart Cry, Can Change Your World   71

#Tears
Sincere Heart Cry, Can Change Your World   71

#Temples
The Mystery of the Temples and Life   140

#The Secret
The Law of Attraction   93

#Thinking
Stop Beating Yourself Up!   38

#Thoughts
Be Careful What You Focus On!   68
Choose Empowering Beliefs   84
First Steps in Reprogramming Your Autopilot   26
Integrity—Live in Truth   116
The Law of Attraction   93
The Voices in our Heads   10
Two Enemies of a Smooth Ride, in the Right Now   63
We Are Meaning Making Machines   24
What Are You Looking For and What Do You Notice?   44
What Is Disease?   33

#Time Freedom
Have You Found Your Golden Goose?   99

#Trust
Perfect Peace in the Midst of a Storm   135
The Tapestry of Life   137

#Truth
Integrity—Live in Truth   116

#Try
No More Trying—Just Do It!   79

#Understanding
The Mystery of Money   97

#Unworthiness
Are Your Gauges of Wealth, Happiness and Success Stuck?   13

#Values
How Much Are You Worth?   5
The Mystery of Money   97
I Am   118

#Victory
Hold On! The Crown, the Fruit, and the Rewards Are On Their Way!   50

#Vision
An Adventure in Goal Setting   127
Are You Planning Your Life?   109
Have You Created a Vision Board?   130
How Do You See the World?   132

#Voices
How Much Are You Worth?   5
What Does It Take to Become Free?   59
Your Spacecraft   4

#Void
Void, Nothingness, or a Place of Loving Energy?   144

#Wealth
Are Your Gauges of Wealth, Happiness and Success Stuck?   13

Have You Found Your Golden Goose?   99
The Mystery of Money   97
The Pursuit of Happiness   103

#Will
No More Trying—Just Do It!   79

#Wisdom
The Pursuit of Happiness   103

#Works
Working Your Way to Heaven Won't Work!   47

INDEX

A

abundance 51, 99
achievement 68, 94, 102, 125
action 7-8, 26, 34, 38, 41-2, 44-5,
    59, 63, 67-9, 74-5, 78-81, 87,
    91, 101, 109
affirmations 26-7, 31, 34, 70,
    118, 123
age 8, 15, 44, 103, 106, 111, 114,
    140-1
Aladdin Factor, The (Canfield and
    Hansen) 199
Alchemist, The (Coelho) 199
Ali, Shamila 49
Allen, James 198
angels xvii, 51, 71, 95
anger 68, 135, 151
anointing 95
answer xvii-xviii, 20, 47, 53,
    57, 71-4, 76, 82, 90, 122,
    153, 155
Anthony, Robert 13
anxiety 44
appreciation 45, 125
archetypes 11, 16
As a Man Thinketh (Allen) 198
association 82-3
attitude 17-18, 37, 41, 45, 53, 56,
    62, 98, 122, 145
autopilot 2, 7, 9, 17-20, 26

Awaken the Giant Within
    (Robbins) 199
awakening 89, 132, 143, 150-
    1, 155

B

balance 24-5, 67, 75, 80, 93, 146
being xx, 1, 5, 11, 33, 42-3, 59,
    71-4, 77-8, 88-9, 105-6, 111,
    140, 142-4, 148-52
beliefs 4, 9-10, 13, 18-19, 25-7,
    29-31, 36-7, 39, 41-2, 56-7,
    59, 61-2, 73-4, 89-90, 142-4
believe 18-19, 30, 35-6, 39, 56,
    65, 74, 78-9, 82, 95, 107,
    109, 114, 121, 148-9
Bhagavad-Gita xvii
Bible xvii-xviii, 38, 89, 97,
    135, 148
Big Al 7
Biology of Belief, The (Lipton) 200
bitterness 62, 90, 107, 146
blame 24, 56, 85, 113
blocks 30
bodies xiii, xx, 2, 7, 15, 33-4, 67,
    89, 106, 140
broke 5, 116, 118
Brown, Les xx, 200
Buddha 47, 103

burdens   47, 62, 120, 138, 143
Byrne, Rhonda   198, 200

C

Campbell, Joseph   24
Canfield, Jack   30, 199
Carnegie, Dale   199
Carroll, Amy   135
causes   36, 41, 45, 56, 153
centre   1, 23, 56-8, 78, 120, 151
change   12-13, 18, 25, 34, 36, 39-40, 45, 53, 69, 73-6, 81-2, 89-91, 133-4, 148, 199
Change Your Thinking, Change Your Life (Tracy)   199
chatter   5, 16, 26, 66
cheating   116
children   xviii, 5, 40, 66, 89, 103, 145
choices   xii, xviii, 8, 17, 19, 21, 26, 29-31, 43-4, 81, 87, 96, 99, 146, 149-50
Churchill, Winston   39, 50, 82
circumstances   45, 75, 109, 126, 135-6
Cisneros, James Blanchard   89
cleansing   43, 73, 78, 107-8
clearing   115
Coelho, Paulo   56, 199
comfort   13, 120
comfort zone   12, 127-8
commander   17, 23, 89
commitment   xix, 74, 76, 80, 90-1, 112, 122, 130
committed   42, 44, 78, 108
communication   57-8, 79
compassion   42, 86, 96
complaint   34, 44
confidence   18, 57, 72, 79, 86, 199
conformity   12-14, 105, 134
connection   41-2, 49, 105, 112-14, 123, 153
conscience   81

conscious mind   7, 68, 128
consciousness   xvi-xvii, 2, 31, 44, 52, 77, 105, 144
consequences   49, 87
control   2, 4, 11, 13-18, 23, 26-7, 31-2, 37, 41, 55-7, 61-2, 65, 69, 72, 84-5
Conversations with God (Walsch)   198
Cox, Billy   77
Crippen, Creig   114
cures   34

D

damnation   82, 104
darkness   32, 34, 71, 73, 78, 83, 88-9, 146
dating   xxi, 114
Davis, Thema   41
death   25, 51, 68, 78, 89, 132, 141-3, 146, 150-1, 153
decisions   xiii, 4, 7-8, 12, 16-18, 26, 31, 38, 41, 43, 49, 51, 75-6, 116-17, 128
Demartini, Dr John   78
desires   xviii-xxi, 10, 14, 16, 21, 42-3, 52, 57, 67-8, 70-6, 90, 94-5, 128-31, 144, 152-3
despair   2, 116, 143
destiny   12, 19, 52, 74, 112, 129
determination   23, 50, 74, 129
detox   67
devil   97, 105
direction   vii, xiii, xvii-xviii, 2, 14, 16-17, 19-20, 24, 26-7, 56, 59, 69, 71, 116-17, 129
disappointment   xv, 9, 40
discouragement   137-8
disease   33-4, 36, 63, 69
Disney, Walt   130
dissatisfaction   34
divine   105-6, 140, 144, 148
doctor   35-6

dream   9-10, 18-19, 47, 51, 67, 71,
    78, 94-5, 99, 102, 109, 122,
    127-30, 132, 143
driving   44
Dwoskin, Hale   30, 199
Dyer, Wayne   xx, 45, 61, 118, 142,
    150, 198
Dynamic Laws of Prosperity, The
    (Ponder)   199

E

earth   xiii, 5, 39, 111, 114, 121,
    125-6, 129, 148, 150-1
effort   xx, 65, 74-5, 100-1, 117,
    123, 137
EFT   36
ego   13, 15-16, 23, 61, 65, 107,
    136, 150
Einstein, Albert   57
Eker, Harv T.   xx, 199
Ellison, Ralph   74
emotions   17, 24, 33, 62-3, 66, 68,
    96, 122, 144, 151
empowered   12, 77, 95
empowerment   95
energy   xxi, 2, 5, 33-4, 36-7, 42,
    63-4, 82, 84, 88, 97-8, 105,
    128-9, 141-4, 148-50
enjoyment   109, 142
enlightenment   47, 89, 144
eternal life   150
eternity   25, 142
expectation   36, 57, 145
experiences   1-2, 11-12, 33, 38-
    45, 49, 59-60, 65-8, 71-2,
    77-8, 88-9, 105-7, 110-11,
    113-15, 142-4, 149-52

F

failure   5, 13, 18, 24, 35, 39-41,
    54, 56, 74, 80, 83, 87, 125,
    127, 137
faith   viii, 19, 48, 50-2, 57, 72, 75,
    79, 94, 98, 132, 135-7
fears   4, 8, 12-14, 18, 20, 28-31,
    41-3, 57-8, 63-6, 72, 77-9,
    88-91, 104-6, 136, 150-1
Feel the Fear and Do it Anyway
    (Jeffers)   200
feelings   8-9, 13, 26, 29, 33-4, 38,
    46-7, 61, 84, 90, 94, 97, 109,
    116, 120
Fine, Randi G.   142
fix   2, 45, 48, 66, 146
flow   x-xi, 20, 31, 33, 36, 40, 51,
    61, 80, 88, 98, 100, 108, 131
fly   xiii, xvii, 1, 14, 16-19, 23, 28-
    30, 41, 44, 59-60, 62, 78-9,
    103, 105, 124-5
focus   44-5, 63, 65, 68, 73, 84,
    93, 118, 128, 136, 153
Fogg, John Milton   45, 199
Ford, Arielle   xxi, 199
Ford, Henry   23, 87
forever   18, 32, 47, 83, 86, 143-
    4, 153
forgiveness   47, 61-2, 77-8, 90,
    107-8
Fourth Wise Man, The   146
free   xi, xiv, 1, 12, 20, 24, 35, 51,
    59, 73, 103-4, 143
freedom   xx, 43, 62, 88, 99-102,
    105, 122, 128, 142
  financial   99-102, 122
friends   xix, 13, 31, 155, 199
frustration   2, 138
future   10, 28, 63-5, 75-6, 90,
    94, 100, 120, 123, 131, 137,
    149, 153

G

game   xii, 20, 43, 53, 90, 103,
   122, 153
genius   134
Gilbert, Rob   7
give   xii, 2, 13, 27, 29-30, 35, 39,
   42, 70-1, 75-6, 95, 97-8,
   128-9, 145-6, 153-4
giving   xviii, 9, 51, 56, 75, 102,
   140, 145-6, 149, 154-5
goals   xix-xx, 18, 45, 50, 71, 99,
   102, 125, 127, 129-30
God   xvii-xviii, 82, 97, 118, 140-1,
   148-50, 153, 197-8
Goddard, Neville   199
Golden Goose   xix, 99-101
grateful   8, 34, 98
gratification   146
gratitude   34, 45-6, 48, 54, 63-5,
   69, 77, 82, 96, 145
Gray, John   xxi
*The Greatest Networker in the
   World* (Fogg)   199
grief   11, 45
growth   ix, xi, xiii, xx-xxi, 12, 39-
   40, 43, 49, 51, 101-2, 112-13,
   117, 120, 122-3, 155
guidebook   xiii, 109
guides   95, 111

H

habits   xiii, 6-7, 14, 16, 24, 27,
   31, 33-4, 38, 45, 59, 67, 69,
   74, 96
Hale, Mandy   12
Hansen, Mark Victor   199
happiness   3, 13, 35, 38, 56, 63,
   84-5, 91, 96, 103, 120
happy   34, 38, 56, 70, 79,
   103, 200
Happy for No Reason
   (Shimoff)   200

hate   38, 151
Hawaiian   47
Hay, Louise   28, 86, 198
healing   xxi, 33-4, 36-7, 47, 53, 75,
   78, 89, 121, 148
health   xxi, 62, 84-5, 91
heart   1, 15, 19, 35, 39, 43, 52-3,
   69, 71, 108-9, 112, 114, 120,
   136, 140
heart cry   69, 71-4, 78
heaven   47, 104, 125, 149-52
hell   56, 82, 134, 148
helpers   95
Hill, Napoleon   xx, 96, 198
hindering   9, 30
Holden, Robert   vii, 86, 198
Holt, Victoria   38
honour   23
Ho'oponopono   47, 77-8
hope   xiii, xxi, 56, 69, 71, 112,
   116, 137
How   xi, xvii, 2, 5, 7, 13, 17, 25, 34,
   45, 56-7, 79, 99-101, 105-6,
   153-4
*How to Win Friends and Influence
   People* (Carnegie)   199
Howard, Christopher   xx
human   1, 15, 24, 33, 41-2, 47, 50,
   61, 65, 68-9, 77, 107, 142,
   150-1, 197
humiliated   41
humiliation   41
Huxley, Aldous   xvii

I

ideals   109
illness   xx, 150
illusion   31
imagination   20, 28
improve   45
indecision   38, 79, 87
information   ii, 16, 66, 87, 128
injustice   107

inner child   11, 15-16, 42
insanity   132, 134
integrity   80, 102, 116
intentions   14, 26-7, 57, 69, 82-3,
    131, 198

J

jealousy   13, 148
Jeffers, Susan   200
journey   xi-xv, xx-xxi, 1, 15-16, 25,
    37-9, 42-4, 62, 87-8, 103-4,
    112-15, 125-7, 142-3, 148-
    51, 155
judgement   61
Jung, Carl   11

K

Kiyosaki, Robert   xx, 5, 199
Koran   xvii

L

Lao Tzu   2, 63
laughter   47
Law of Attraction   xx, 57, 93-
    4, 122
learnings   xiii, xx, 53, 122
Leary, Timothy   xvii
Len, Dr Ihaleakala Hew   77
lessons   xiii, xxi, 39-40, 45, 47,
    100, 102, 112, 122, 129, 139,
    145-6, 155
Letting go   30, 75
Lewis, C. S.   116
life   ix-xi, xvii, 15, 24-6, 29-30, 32,
    34, 47-8, 65, 86, 120-1, 126-
    7, 137-8, 140-4, 198-200
Life Loves You (Hay, Holden)   198
light   xvii, 2, 32, 54, 73, 78, 86,
    88-9, 105, 110, 136, 141

limiting beliefs   13, 20, 59, 90, 97,
    105, 115
Lipton, Bruce   200
listen   13, 20, 53, 57, 75, 128,
    132, 153
Living an Inspired Life (Rohn)   198
lonely   42, 86, 112, 125-6, 148
Loren, Sophia   132
loss   24, 39, 64, 68, 102, 120-1,
    123, 142-3
love   vii, ix-x, xx-xxi, 14-15, 31, 41-
    3, 47-8, 77-8, 89-90, 105-8,
    112-13, 124-6, 136, 141-2,
    145-50
lying   116

M

machine   xvi, 4, 85
madness   132, 134
Man of La Mancha   132
Mandela, Nelson   62
Manifest Your Destiny (Dyer)   198
manifestation   20, 29, 33, 35, 94,
    114, 130, 151
manual   2, 101, 126
Maté, Gabor   4
Maxwell, John C.   109
meaning   24, 26, 49, 53, 78, 80,
    86, 112, 137, 140, 147
medicine   36
mediocrity   12, 18, 127, 129
meditation   15, 47, 67, 136
Meet Dave   200
memories   xvi, 50, 63
Merton, Thomas   112
millionaire   102, 126, 199
Millman, Dan   97
mind   135, 199
mindfulness   26, 77, 93
miracle   34-5, 45, 64, 69, 72-3,
    82, 117, 136, 151
Mirdad, Michael   88, 199
mission   vii, 23, 57, 104

MLM   101
modalities   34, 36, 136, 148
money   97-8, 100-2, 109, 116, 122
mood   24, 46
mountain   12, 50, 112, 139
mourning   142
Murphy, Joseph   93
music   xvi
Myss, Caroline   36
mysteries   111, 140

N

need   vii, 14, 42, 58, 85, 145, 150
network marketing   101
new beginnings   121
news   63, 66-7, 69, 74, 156
Nightingale, Earl   xx, 66, 198
NLP   xx-xxi
nothingness   144
now   xviii-xxi, 4-5, 7-8, 12-13, 15-
      16, 24-5, 29, 34, 41, 51, 63-
      6, 71, 120-1, 144-6, 151
Nudity   105

O

observer   10, 26, 31, 53, 78, 144
Olsen, Jeff   200
oneness   112
O'Toole, Peter   132

P

passion   xix, 11, 133, 150, 153
past   ix, 8, 10, 14, 31, 38, 42-4,
      62-4, 76, 86, 88, 90, 111-12,
      120, 135-6
past lives   111
peace   10, 33, 62-3, 82, 107, 135-
      6, 153
Peerless, April   33
perfection   25, 47, 73, 139

persistence   27, 50, 133, 153
personalities   11, 15
personality types   11
Pilgrim, Peace   10
pilot   11, 17-18, 56, 79, 86
pleasure   xix, 38, 50, 70, 105-6,
      113, 120, 122, 140, 150, 152
Ponder, Catherine   199
power   5-6, 8, 17, 19, 28, 30-1, 65,
      68-9, 77-8, 82-3, 91, 140-1,
      148, 150-1, 198-9
Power of Awareness, The
      (Goddard)   199
Power of Intention, The
      (Dyer)   198
Power of Now, The (Tolle)   199
practice   17, 26-7, 30, 47, 77, 82,
      86, 117-18
prayer   xvii, 72, 77-8, 82-3,
      91, 108
procrastination   138
Proctor, Bob   xx, 84, 198
programming   16, 18, 26-7, 41, 67,
      93, 125
purpose   xvii-xviii, xx, 23, 51-2,
      54, 65, 68-9, 71, 73-4, 79,
      82, 91, 127-8, 137, 140

Q

Quantum Physics   xx
Quantum Touch   36
questions   xiii, xvii, xx, 7, 20, 28,
      30, 45, 53, 57, 74-5, 90, 122,
      153, 155-6
quiet   13, 20, 53, 57, 67, 71-2, 90,
      95, 120-1, 129, 136
Quixote, Don   132
quotes   27, 53, 156

TAKE CONTROL OF YOUR SPACECRAFT AND FLY BACK TO LOVE

R

RAS (reticular activation
  system) 128
reality xvii, 13, 24, 27-8, 34, 56,
  64, 68, 76, 93, 109, 130,
  132, 142
realm 31, 94, 120, 150-2, 154
reason 24, 127
Reiki 36, 66-7
rejection 41, 54
relationship xix, 18, 29, 75,
  125, 145
release 86
religion xiii, 4, 16, 47, 61, 82, 103,
  105, 140
remember xv-xvi, 23, 31-2, 34,
  38, 45, 47, 57, 59, 61, 64, 78,
  88-9, 111, 136-7
remorse 38, 63
reprogramme 2, 4, 8-9, 27, 42,
  45, 56, 86
respect 61, 116, 125
responsibility 4, 17, 56, 78, 96
responsible 4, 56, 62, 90
results 7, 30, 50, 52, 69, 75, 91,
  94, 123, 134
Return to Love, A
  (Williamson) 199
revenge 62-3, 107
review 20, 27, 53, 90, 119, 122,
  153, 155
rewards 50-2, 146
Rich Dad, Poor Dad
  (Kiyosaki) 199
rituals 47, 54
Robbins, Tony xx, 85, 99, 199
Rohn, Jim xix-xx, 50, 102, 116,
  126, 198
roles 11, 15, 23, 149
root 34, 41, 63, 68, 70, 107, 149
routine 12, 47, 67, 101, 132
Rowling, J. K. 18
Rumi 71, 88, 120, 140

S

sacrifice 145-6
sad 43, 69, 82, 99, 120, 125-6,
  128, 138
Schreiter, Tom 7
Science of Getting Rich, The
  (Wattles) 198
Science of Self Confidence, The
  (Tracy) 199
Secret, The (Byrne) xx, 93,
  198-200
Secret of the Millionaire Mind, The
  (Eker) 199
Sedona Method, The (Dwoskin)
  30, 199
self 19, 56, 107-8, 131, 146, 199
self-confidence 19, 61
self-doubt 138-9
self-love 19, 116
self-righteousness 45, 47, 61
Seneca 134
sex 105-6
Shimoff, Marci 200
should xix, 25, 47, 67, 79, 81, 91,
  98, 102, 107, 118, 127-8, 132
Sinclair, Adlin 137
Slight Edge, The (Olsen) 200
solution 36, 48, 62, 135
soul xvii, 28, 36, 67, 120, 129, 199
soul mate xx-xxi, 112, 114
Soulmate Secret, The (Ford) 199
Spacecraft xiii-xv, 1, 4-5, 7, 11,
  18, 23, 27, 36-8, 42, 56, 86,
  89, 126, 142-3
spirit x-xi, xiii, xviii-xx, 19, 25, 40,
  57, 62, 65, 79, 90, 95-6, 111,
  151-3, 197
spirit guide 111
storms 26, 29, 72, 75, 121, 135
Strangest Secret, The
  (Nightingale) 198
stress 15
stressed 34
strong 11, 13, 16, 41, 59, 119

struggle   88, 91
stuck   xxi, 3, 13, 18, 30, 33-4, 36,
         49, 63-5, 75, 96, 101, 103,
         109, 128-9
subconscious mind   20
success   vii, xv, xx, 3, 8-9, 12-13,
         23, 29, 36, 39, 50, 52, 56,
         116, 125-9
Success Principles, The
         (Canfield)   199
Swayne, Clinton   xx

T

Tao Te Ching   15
Taylor, Anna   82
Teamwork   23
tears   xvii-xviii, 71-4, 86, 120, 138
temples   120, 140
tested   52, 84, 135
Think and Grow Rich (Hill)   198
thinking   7, 24, 38, 94, 199
thoughts   xii-xiii, 10, 23-4, 26-8,
         31, 33-6, 63-4, 67-70, 78,
         81-2, 84, 93-4, 108-9, 117-
         19, 130-2
time   xi-xiii, 4-7, 23-5, 33-5, 51-4,
         59-67, 69-72, 81, 86-7, 99-
         101, 108-12, 119-23, 125-32,
         137-8, 150-5
Tolle, Eckhart   144
tools   15, 30, 34, 77, 197
Tracy, Brian   xx, 59, 68, 199
transformation   34-5, 136
trials   73, 138
troubles   31, 45, 64, 137, 150
trust   vii, xiii, xxi, 35, 53, 65, 87,
         93-4, 120, 137, 155
truth   xxi, 1, 31, 35, 39, 43, 47, 78,
         89, 116, 128, 136, 140-3,
         148-9, 152
try   79
Twain, Mark   29

U

Uchtdorf, Dieter F.   125
unconscious mind   30
understanding   xx, 49, 90, 95, 120
universe   xvi, 31, 34, 50, 52,
         71, 78, 93, 105, 118, 131,
         140, 145
unlimited   43, 148
unworthiness   13-14, 47
Unwrap Your Infinite Greatness
         (Brown)   200

V

values   xix, 5, 61, 67, 70, 97-8,
         100-2, 118, 126, 146, 150-1
victory   31, 52, 72, 83, 125
vision   xx, 17, 120, 130, 133,
         139, 153
vision board   128, 130-1, 153
visualise   29, 94, 132
Vitale, Joe   77, 199
voices   xviii, xxi, 4-6, 10, 26, 35,
         38, 45, 53, 59, 61, 72, 81, 86
void   77, 144
voyage   xxi, 1, 5-6, 13, 38-9, 59,
         65, 82, 89, 109, 127, 142-3

W

wake   xiii, 2, 7, 63, 88, 142
Walsch, Neale Donald   198
Washington, Denzel   145
Wattles, Wallace   xx, 198
wealth   3, 13, 48, 61, 67, 84-5, 91,
         99-100, 103, 145
weights   34, 44, 62
well   1-2, 5, 11, 18, 33-4, 37, 39,
         64, 72, 76, 80, 94, 100, 103,
         135-6
what if Game   xii, 20, 53, 90,
         122, 153

What the Bleep? Down the Rabbit Hole 200

Wilde, Oscar 105

will 10-11, 28, 30-3, 37-9, 50-3, 61-2, 69-72, 76-80, 86-8, 98-100, 102-3, 109-10, 114-16, 135-6, 155-6

Williamson, Marianne 107, 199

Winfrey, Oprah 31

wisdom xiii, xx-xxi, 65, 93, 95, 103, 114

within xiii, xvii, xxi, 11, 23, 32, 52, 71-3, 77, 86, 89, 99, 107, 140-1, 197-9

works 47-8, 197-8

writing xix, 57, 59, 119, 131

Y

Yoda 79

You are Not Going Crazy, You are Just Waking Up (Mirdad) 199

You Were Born Rich (Proctor) 198

You'll see It When You Believe It (Dyer) 198

Z

Zero Limits (Vitale) 199

RECOMMENDED BOOKS, AUDIO PROGRAMMES, MENTORS, AND MOVIES

These are just some of the books and tools that have been a part of my journey. The list would be too long and my memory not exhaustive enough to contain all the powerful works that have moved me, ever onwards in this amazing journey of life. You will find certain books call and speak to you too!

I would heartily recommend making the time, in your daily activities, to read at least six pages of a good, feeding, and inspiring book every day. As you seek wisdom and Love, you will find Spirit will lead you to the right teachers, in many wonderful ways. 'When the student is ready, the teacher will come.' Remember though, that all of these teachers are just human and also on their paths, maybe in some areas, are just a bit ahead of you. However, they are also just like you—men or women of passion and likewise may be far from enlightened in every area. Weigh each truth you hear in your own beautiful heart and decide if it feels right for you and for now. It may save you from falling into the trap of yet another religion or man-worship, rather than seeing another human on their own path with wise words to share and acknowledging that part of Spirit and God within them. Namaste.

We stand on the shoulders and wisdom of the giants that have gone before us; many of them have been a part of our collective wisdom and awakening process. Passed on from them, there are many great works and signposts that are blazing a trail forward and contain great truths. Yet I believe the ultimate truths are to be found inside us—as we awaken to the realisation that we are a part of the All, and the very breath of Life itself.

As a Man Thinketh – James Allen

Think and Grow Rich – Napoleon Hill

The Strangest Secret – Earl Nightingale

You Were Born Rich – Bob Proctor; and his audio class: Born Rich

Many of the Audios and Books by Jim Rohn especially: *Living an Inspired Life*

Wayne Dyer. -- I have read most of his books. Especially powerful are:

The Power of Intention – Wayne Dyer

Manifest Your Destiny – Wayne Dyer

You'll See it When You Believe it – Wayne Dyer

The Science of Getting Rich – Wallace Wattles

Life Loves You – Louise Hay and Robert Holden

Conversations with God – Series – Neale Donald Walsch

The Secret – Rhonda Byrne. – And many of the books from the teachers who shared their knowledge within

Change Your Thinking, Change Your Life – Brian Tracy. – And his audio class: *The Science of Self Confidence*

The Power of Awareness – Neville Goddard

Rich Dad, Poor Dad – Robert Kiyosaki

The Dynamic Laws of Prosperity – Catherine Ponder

The Alchemist and many great books by Paulo Coelho

The Secret of the Millionaire Mind – T Harv Eker. – And his workshop by the same name

Zero Limits – Joe Vitale

The Greatest Networker in the World – John Milton Fogg

How to Win Friends and Influence People – Dale Carnegie

The Sedona Method – Hale Dwoskin

The Success Principles – Jack Canfield

The Aladdin Factor – Jack Canfield and Mark Victor Hansen

A Return to Love – Marianne Williamson

You are Not Going Crazy, You are Just Waking Up – The Five Stages of the Soul Transformation Process – Michael Mirdad

Awaken the Giant Within – Tony Robbins

The Power of Now – Ekhart Tolle

The Soulmate Secret – Arielle Ford

Happy for No Reason – Marci Shimoff

Life Visioning – Michael Bernard Beckwith

The Biology of Belief – Bruce Lipton

The Slight Edge – Jeff Olsen

Feel the Fear and Do it Anyway – Susan Jeffers

Unwrap Your Infinite Greatness – Audio – Les Brown

Movies

The Secret - Rhonda Byrne - Movie

What the Bleep? Down the Rabbit Hole – Movie

Meet Dave – Comedy – Movie

ABOUT THE AUTHOR

Keith Higgs has lived an interesting and exceptional life.

A hippie search for truth; twenty years of International Christian-based voluntary work; Editing and publishing talks and inspirational audios; Building a successful computer business—then watching it crash; Two marriages, eight children and six stepchildren; Building a MLM business, Learning from the masters of personal growth; Attending and assisting at talks and workshops; Studying NLP, healing and speaking skills; Building a social media platforms of thousands; Travelling many countries.

His combined skills, common sense, learnings and accumulated wisdom have flowed into 'Take Control of Your Spacecraft and Fly Back to Love - a Manual and Guidebook for Life's Journey.'

Here is a man who has lived and learnt. He has a passion to share his truths, values, and beliefs with many.